TURN OF THE CENTURY

Turn Of The Century

by Albert Britt

BARRE PUBLISHERS
BARRE, MASSACHUSETTS
1966

Copyright © 1966 by Barre Publishers
Library of Congress Catalogue Card Number 66-23205
Composed and Printed in the United States of America

To Tommy

In memory of our long friendship

CONTENTS

INTRODUCTION

"TURN of the Century" is a mixture of chronicle and comment. It makes no boast of originality or finality. It is the result of a long look back from this year of 1966 — history as one man sees it. In effect it is a sequel or continuation of "An America That Was."

New York in 1898 had lately become one of the great cities of the world by an act of municipal necromancy, turning counties into boroughs under a single mayor. Street traffic was confused and changing as it still is. The horse was the chief motive power, but electricity and motors were coming fast. The streets were foul and fit only for the adventures of English sparrows. Small steam engines hauled overcrowed rattling trains along elevated railroads; talk was heard of subways. Cable cars were operating on Broadway and on Lexington Avenue. Fifth Avenue and Madison were sacred to the mansions of the Four Hundred — but not for long. To a boy from the West it was exciting, friendless and homeless.

After graduating from college I left immediately for New York City which was to be my home for twenty-seven years. In that time, I did many things — editing magazines, writing and publishing books — and knew many people. I knew S. S. McClure as well as it was possible to know that unpredictable genius. I served on the staff of Frank Munsey's magazine factory. He was a money maker, not a genius. I knew Theodore Roosevelt as thousands knew him, a leading figure in a political melodrama.

Now, reminiscing in my old age, this is the way things look to me. It was an exciting time to be alive, and I was young then.

ALBERT BRITT

Wellington Farm
Nonquitt, Mass.
April, 1966

vii

FOREWORD

THE writer of a foreword to a good book — a somewhat unnecessary adjunct — should no doubt focus his remarks exclusively on its author and contents. I am tempted to depart in some measure from this obligation.

Albert Britt, my friend of long standing, is more than a decade my senior in both years and wisdom. The events which he so vividly chronicles here were part and parcel of his experiences as an active participant in the journalism of a great city. To me they were hazy incidents, far removed from the life of a schoolboy in a small southern town.

But as I read the galley proofs of this fascinating book, many memories, forgotten or dimly remembered, come alive. Again I am curled in a corner poring over Ida Tarbell's life of Napoleon, with its illustrations showing the gorgeously uniformed Corsican charging into the fray, his sword uplifted, his impeccably groomed steed curveting on its hind legs, its silky mane and tail billowing out behind. This was war! This was romance. Many years later I discovered by personal observation that war is not at all like that.

The Spanish-American War passages bring back a picture of my father and a neighbor gloating across the back fence over news of Admiral Dewey's victory at Manila Bay. As I read I recall memories of a small boy's visit to an army camp in a nearby city, sixteen miles and nearly three hours away, where thousands of blue-clad soldiers are being trained to go against the formidable foe; of swelling with pride when one of our local boys, home on furlough (a sergeant no less) condescends to greet me on the street; of the incredibly sentimental war songs. There was

one about Bluebell searching for her lover among the returning
heroes:

Sadly they tell the story, tell how he fought and fell.

No thought of fame or glory, only of his Bluebell.

I again stand in awe as Teddy the Rough Rider, his rumpled
black Stetson crushed in his fist, delivers an impassioned ha-
rangue from the portico of the county court house. My amazement knew no bounds when he mentioned by name some of our
legendary local heroes; John Sevier, Sam Houston, David Glasgow Farragut, "Parson" Brownlow. No suspicion that he had
been coached beforehand by a local politician ever entered my
mind.

I recall my vicarious pride in the exploit of Richmond Pearson Hobson in sinking the *Merrimac* in the narrow entrance to
Santiago Harbor, a shining example of daredeviltry that was
somewhat dimmed later when the Spanish fleet steamed blithely
around the wreck.

Long forgotten but now recalled are the youthful titilla-
tions occasioned by the mildly explicit reporting of the Harry
Thaw trial; the thrill of reading Mary Johnston's "To Have and
to Hold", Walter D. Edmonds', "Drums Along the Mohawk",
George Ade's "Fables in Slang", and above all, the delight of my
first reading of "Huckleberry Finn".

All these and many other shadowy memories have been
revived by this books' evocation of the events of long ago. But to
thoroughly enjoy these pages, a reader need not have lived through
the period of our history that they so wonderfully describe. Whether you are young or old, "Turn of the Century" will present
an engrossing picture of the times before we had taken upon ourselves the vexations and frustrations that beset a world power.

My path crossed Bert Britt's soon after I came insecurely
to roost in New York in 1920. We were both courting girls who
lived together in a small apartment on Madison Square. Both

our suits came to successful conclusions. My most valued heritage from this association — next after the acquisition of a wife — is a friendship that has been cherished ever since. I value it even more highly now after having had the privilege of reading this memorable book.

Carl Burger,
Pleasantville, New York

CHAPTER I

New York As It Was

"AT THE turn of the century?" That was a familiar phrase in the late nineties, but just when did the century turn? Was it December 31, 1899, or a year later? If there are a hundred years in a century, ours must have ended with the year 1900. Obvious as that seems, there was strong and voluble support for 1899 as the last year of the dying century. Editorials were written about it. The more excited, or articulate, wrote letters to the editor, clergymen dealt with it in their sermons as though there was an orthodox position on the habits of centuries. Then, in spite of all the silly argument, the century ended and the world continued to revolve.

The period since the Civil War had been a time of rapid change and to the lucky ones great progress. Henry Adams summed it up in his *Education of Henry Adams*: "In the essentials like religion, ethics, philosophy; in literature, history, art; in the concepts of all the sciences, except perhaps mathematics, the American boy of 1854 stood nearer the year one than the year 1900." If that was true what was left for us to do? When the generation in college in the late ninetes thought about the world into which we were soon to step, we saw it as substantially the world our fathers had known, better and brighter for our coming, of course, but in pace and form little different from what it had been. Only a few wild dreamers, the Marconis, the Edisons, the Wrights, and Teslas had an inkling of the truth that the world would never be the same again.

1

When I look back from this year 1965, I have a feeling of
proprietorship in that turn of the century. It belonged to me by
a vague right of discovery. It was in 1898, a year of war, that I
graduated from college and went to New York where I was to
live for more than twenty-five years. Big cities were something
new in my experience. I had been in Chicago once or twice for a
few days at a time, but that didn't really count as experience. For
me, that trip to New York was a venture into the unknown. The
route I took was obvious enough at the beginning, Chicago, De-
troit, Niagara Falls, but beyond that there were such towns as
Rome, Watertown, Ogdensburg, Kingston-on-the-Hudson, ang-
ling down across the state. By the time I reached Kingston I
had seen more little villages than I had supposed existed, each
with its cemetery whose inhabitants seemed to far outnumber the
living. I grudged the time for dozing as I sat with my eyes glued
to the window staring at the picturesque countryside in no way
resembling the flat lands of Illinois. Here were small houses,
white churches with tall steeples, everywhere the signs of age.
These people thought in term of generations and centuries instead
of the years and decades of Illinos, and I couldn't see enough of it.
And the cost of all that wide wandering? Nineteen dollars and
ninety-seven cents.

That first summer in New York was a time of celebrations
of victory over the Spanish and I saw the parade down Riverside
Drive and Fifth Avenue in honor of our returning heroes. I saw
Theodore Roosevelt riding among his Rough Riders. I saw Richard Croker riding in his carriage with city notables and I noted
the grim smile with which he greeted the boos that followed him
along the route. He really had a tiger look.

New York had just become one of the great cities of the
world by dint of turning the counties of Manhattan, Queens,
Brooklyn, the Bronx, and Richmond into boroughs to make Greater New York under a single mayor in line with the prevalent wor-
ship of size. Outwardly the city that one saw was more old than
new. Horse cars were in common use and were to continue for

a long time to come. Electric trolleys were coming in to compete with horses for the right of way and it was the hard luck of Amsterdam Avenue to be especially vulnerable. Here was a broad avenue on the west side much used and lined with small shops and low-priced apartment houses. The temptation was too strong to be resisted and two companies had moved in, one a trolley line the other horse drawn.

Soon the horse car outfit announced that the traffic potential was so promising that the substitution of electricity for horses was about to begin. This was free enterprise with a vengeance. For a simple pedestrian to cross Amsterdam Avenue with four trolley lines roaring and banging down on him would have been like asking him to swim the rapids below Niagara. That it didn't happen was to the credit of one man, the Rev. John Peters, rector of St. Michaels, a large Episcopal church on the avenue. The Rev. John was a little fighting terrier of a man who could be counted on to hold fast once he got his teeth in. Sunday after Sunday, and in between, he rang the changes on the cruel stupidity of the proposed change and, faced with the outraged public sentiment whipped up by the Rev. John, the corporation changed its collective mind and soon abandoned the avenue altogether.

Cable cars were operating on Broadway and on Lexington Avenue. Expensive to install and maintain, limited to the cable speed of eight miles an hour, they were destined to be short lived. There were danger spots along the line. One at the southwest corner of Union Square was known as "Dead Man's Curve" where the operator had to take the turn at top speed or lose his hold on the cable altogether.

In downtown sections where traffic was heaviest, cobblestone pavements were the rule with asphalt appearing on such thoroughfares as Fifth and Madison Avenue. Chicago was experimenting with wood blocks, but I recall none in New York. Elevated railways dominated the chief north and south avenues, and noisy, dirty, unsightly things they were. The motive power for the trains was provided by stubby little coal-burning locomotives, many of which were exiled to the Panama Canal when work there began. Horses were everywhere and no one took the talk of horseless carriages seriously; at the most only toys for a few daring plutocrats. There were few thrills to match the sight of three fire horses hitched abreast galloping down Fifth Avenue at full stretch, smoke rolling from the stack, sparks flying, firemen clinging to the rails at the side. To have seen that once is to remember it as long as memory remains.

In common with most large American cities, traction in New York was discordant and amorphous. Franchises were granted with little reference to the type of service to be rendered as was the case on Amsterdam Avenue. Transfers were without system or predictability with the result that two or three fares might be required for a relatively short trip, especially when the destinaton involved both crosstown and up or downtown travel. Company was heaped on company in a tangle that kept the courts busy for years. It was the subway that first brought something resembling an orderly system into this corporate jungle.

By pure chance, a savage past came into the subway operation. A station that I was to use aften at Broadway and West 103rd Street had a ticket taker who caught my eye. He was dark and slender and stood erect as a sentry at his post. A bronze service button in the lapel of his coat ultimately led to his identificaton. His name on the payroll of the company was John Martin, more properly Giovanni Martini. He was the bugler that Custer had sent back to order Major Reno and Captain Benteen to come fast to his aid when he had his first real look at the formidable force that the Sioux had brought together on the Little Big Horn for this their last and best fight. Reno and Benteen had their hands full where they were, and so John Martin became the sole survivor of the massacre that slew five troops of the Seventh cavalry, two hundred and seventy-seven officers and men. That had been less than thirty years before I saw him standing at his post in the New York subway.

With the coming of the subway and the passing of the horse

a long-needed change appeared. Attention turned to the need for
clean streets. Hitherto only random attempts at such a move
had been made and busy streets were Augean stables in appearance. When the first steps were taken in the organization of street
cleaning squads, newspaper headlines chortled in derision and
christened the first workers in white uniforms "white wings."
When Col. Charles H. Waring, the head of the new bureau, in-
sisted that place be reserved in a municipal parade for a company of his men in clean white unforms, carrying their brooms as
soldiers carry their guns, derision turned to applause. The street
cleaners had it made.

Electric lights were coming in, but in the older houses illu-
mination was still with gas. Only the well-to-do could afford tele-
phones in their homes. By 1900, the Bell system reported only
677,000 instruments in Greater New York. The present total is
close to seventy million. The typical New York house was the
brown stone front with three stories and a high basement sometimes called "English" basement, usually holding kitchen and
dining room. Often there was a weary looking rubber plant in the
front hall. Apartment houses were growing in number and size
mostly of the "railroad" type with rooms strung along a single
hall like cars in a railroad train. Skyscrapers were unknown
until 1900 when a twenty-nine story building was erected on Park
Row, remembered only as the Syndicate building.

When I first saw New York, Fifth Avenue was still sacred
to the mansions of the rich: Vanderbilts, Sloans, Astors, Schuy-
lers, Rhinelanders, Goelets, all members of the fabled Four Hundred. At the Washington Square end of the avenue marked by
the impressive Washington Arch was the Hotel Brevoort, proud
of its kitchen and its cellar, but at the corner of Thirty-Fourth
Street was a far more impressive and expensive hostelry, the Wal-
dorf-Astoria. On this site the Empire State Building now lifts a
proud head into the air twelve hundred and fifty feet above street
level.

The upper end of the Fifth Avenue that counted was at Fifty-

Ninth Street, although such newly rich as Andrew Carnegie and
Henry Frick were soon to build their stately mansions in that
unexplored north. On the way up, the stroller found a queer structure at the crossroads of Forty-Second, no mansion but a huge
water reservoir, long out of use but looking over the spot where
a public library was soon to appear and destined to be one of the
great institutions of America. The company that had built that
reservoir went back to the early days of the republic, around the
turn of another century, and the company charter gave wide latitude to the institution thus created with banking added to water
supply. The name of Aaron Burr appeared among the incorpo-
rators. Reservoir and aqueduct had long been dry, but not the
bank.

Socially speaking, the climax of the avenue was the gaudy
château that a Vanderbilt had built at the corner of Fifty-Eighth
and Fifth. Early in my process of becoming acquainted with this
bewildering world of Manhattan, this was the scene of the marriage of the young duke of Marlborough to Consuelo Vanderbilt,
not the first nor the last of the international alliances by which
American money had been siphoned off to aid in the refurbishing
of European titles.

Of course it was idle to expect such a bastion of inherited
wealth and privilege as the Fifth Avenue of my distant observing
to stand indefinitely against the growing challenge of trade. Re-
tail shops of more than ordinary consequence were growing increasingly restive. Tiffany, the jewelry center of America, was
waiting on Union Square a short block from Fifth Avenue as was
Brentano, dealer in rare books and expensive sets and other items
of the publisher's art and publishers were looking around. Macmillan was soon to move over and Scribner was looking hungrily
for greener fields. The old house of Harper Bros. was to linger
long in its dingy quarters on Franklin Square in the shadow of
Brooklyn Bridge.

A skyscraper began to sprout in the narrow triangle between
Broadway and Fifth and the appropriately named Flatiron Build-

ing soared twenty stories in the air resembling a great ocean liner pushing her way uptown. Business was on its way and the sons and daughters of the élite looked toward Bar Harbor, Newport and lesser places. In due course these too would pass, but Fifth Avenue was their private preserve no more. Madison Square was usurping the place formerly held by Union Square nine blocks down Broadway. In the southwest corner of Madison Square was the old Fifth Avenue Hotel long the traditional headquarters of New York Republicans. It was in that hotel that a clergyman, the Rev. Mr. Burchard, spokesman of a delegation calling on James G. Blaine, Republican candidate for the presidency in 1884, told the world that the Democratic party was the party of "Rum, Romanism, and Rebellion." Evidently the reverend gentleman hadn't heard that the war was over. New York went Democratic in a big way. Those were the days when the New York *Sun* missed few tidbits and a reporter for the *Sun* pounced on that one.

Diagonally across the square was the original Madison Square Garden, masterpiece of Stanford White and the home of circuses, six-day bicycle races, prize fights, horse shows, dog shows, whatever had need of large space, later to be the arena for the tragic killing of the architect. On the north side of the square was the Yale Club and on the west side was Martin's, one of the luxury restaurants of the day. It was in Martin's that a large-mouthed gentleman made scathing comment on the character and habits of Stephen Crane, author of "The Red Badge of Courage", destined to be a classic, unfortunately choosing Richard Harding Davis as one of his auditors. Davis knew Crane, admired him, and promptly knocked the unwise critic over a table and a couple of chairs.

The turn of the century saw immigration growing steadily, nearly a million a year coming in from the old countries, no longer mostly from Great Britain, Germany, and the Scandinavian countries, but also Poles, Italians, Greeks, Slavs. For the most part we made them welcome. Industry was hungry for their strong bodies and low living standards that would offset the

growing demands of the labor unions. The English speech was
disappearing from the mines and mills of Pensylvania. There
were suggestions here and there that this foreign influx might
make serious change in our racial makeup, but as yet there were
few hints of the need for a more careful screening of the incoming
tide, perhaps a more careful checkup for possible contagious disease. As a rule the newcomers came through the open door and
merged with others of like origin already here.

The lines that Emma Lazarus wrote for the Statue of Liberty on Bedloe's Island in New York harbor make pathetic reading now:

"Give us your tired, your poor,
Your huddled masses yearning to breathe free,
The wretched refuse of your teeming shore,
Send these, the homeless, tempest-tossed to me.
I lift my lamp beside the golden door . . . . "

bitter reminder that this was once the land of hope to the huddled masses of an older world that had no hope to offer; not
altogether reason for pride.

There was growing congestion in Jewish, Greek, and Italian quarters, but we were more interested in the cropping up of
foreign restaurants, Levantine, Italian, Hungarian, serving dishes peculiar to the land from which they had come. Those of us
who must count our pennies with care hailed these additions to
our experience with interest. New York had long known German
restaurants, many of them of small expense. Luchow's at the corner of Fourteenth Street and Fourth Avenue was the best known
of these oldtimers, but Luchow's was a cut above our budgets and
we were more concerned with the little places snuggled into the
basements of old dwelling houses. One of these is remembered
as the "Hole in the Wall." The food was plain and good and the
price fitted our pocketbooks. A standard item on the bill of fare
that I recall was "marinirter hering". Once I asked Gus, our regular waiter, to explain it. Gus fiddled with knives and forks and
then took a chance. "Vy," he said "marinirter hering ist-ist-marin-

irter hering," spoken with an air of triumph. It was there also that we became acquainted with a salubrious hot weather drink "Rhine wine mit seltzer." It was a long drink and a mild one and the price was fifteen cents, "per halb schopen."

Somewhere on the lower East Side, Avenue A perhaps, was the Cafe Boulevard, a favorite dining place when there was a small windfall to celebrate. The food was good, basically French with a Viennese touch, a flavor that soon became familiar, and on lower Lexington Avenue there was a Levantine place that was entirely foreign, a mixture of Greek, Turkish, and Armenian. Whatever a dish was called, "Shishkabob" perhaps, it was certain to be mutton and the desserts were cloyingly sweet. There was a good French restaurant on Sixth Avenue, destined to be a casualty of Prohibition. This was Mouquin's and a cut above the basement type with excellent wine at popular places. It was there that I learned about snails, the huge "escargots de Bourgogne" from the vineyards of Burgundy. Even with the addition of wine, a *grave superieur* was especially recommended, three or four of us could dine there at a dollar or less per person. On the lower West Side, French or Italian fare was to be had, *avec vin*, for fifty or sixty cents and the sour wine they served at least washed down the food.

For us conditioned to the meat and potatoes of the Midwest or the South these mild forays gave us a sense of adventuring in foreign lands and we had no envy of those who dined far more expensively at Delmonico's or Sherry's. Chinatown must not be forgotten and we learned to scorn such touristy dishes as chop suey which is not indigenous to the old Flowery Kingdom. Soon we were ordering dinner "family style" with sweet-sour pork, bamboo sprouts, Chinese noodles, and water chestnuts. As a result of the foreign menus on the back streets of New York in those distant days, Chinese food has high rank in my dietary listing. Even a long gorge in Chinatown produced no internal regets, and you can't say that of meat and potatoes.

On Broadway, not far from Wanamaker's mammoth emporium, was the Vienna Bakery with a coffee house adjunct, a pleasant place to sit for a leisurely half-hour over a cup of coffee and hot Vienna roll — and don't spare the butter. The Brevoort on lower Fifth Avenue, where Henry Brevoort had had his farm in the day when Washington Square was a potter's field, offered the best in French dishes as did the Cafe Lafayette a block away. This one gave us a Parisian touch with a game room where we could sip an aperitif and amuse ourselves with dominoes or checkers and savor the illusion of foreign travel.

These places were for high days and holidays when pockets were well lined. The same held true for the chop houses of that day, Parrish far downtown, Engel's, Keene's, Browne's on or near Broadway just below Forty-Second Street. The chop house specialty was a huge English mutton chop and a baked potato. Such chops are no longer to be found in the places of my present frequenting. *Eheu fugaces labuntur anni!*

A feature of New York that was entirely new and endlessly fascinating to a boy from the Midwest was the delicatessen. These were generally German or Italian, sometimes kosher, but whatever the nationality the wide variety of foods offered was irresistible. Cold meats, sausage, salami (always in the Italian), cheese, pickles, jam, potato salad, pickled pigs' feet, sliced ham, cold chicken, sometimes light wine, these and more offered a bewildering choice of appetizing viands ready to serve without the bother of cooking. It was something that our home towns knew not. The delicatessen was far from economical as hard pressed family budgets knew all too well.

The rôtisserie was an institution presumably imported from France. In the window a fowl turning alluringly on a spit, sending forth rich odors on a chilly winter day, invited the passerby to drop in and sample the wares. One rôtisserie that I came to know well made a specialty of delicious turkey hash as a postscript to Thanksgiving and Christmas.

Newcomers were not long in finding their way to Coney Island, and on a hot Sunday afternoon in midsummer sidewheel steamers took us down the bay to a crowded beach for a first acquaintance with ocean breeze. (I did that very thing on my first Sunday in the big city.) Coney Island's specialty was the "shore dinner," somewhat resembling the clam bakes that early settlers learned about from the Indians of Long Island and New England. Salt water, fish, lobsters, clams steamed or in chowder were a revelation to us greenhorns of the west.

I soon discovered that I had something to learn about kinds of food with which I had thought I was quite familiar. For us westerners, beef was an important item in our diet, sometimes roasted, sometimes boiled. We were proud of the quality of our beef and rightly so. Only Simpson's on the Strand in London can match it. But it was our fixed belief that beef must be cooked within an inch of its life. Our roasts should have no red showing and steaks should be cut as thin as possible, then pounded to make them tender and fried over a hot fire. In New York we encountered rare roast beef and thick juicy steaks and learned to like them.

My first Christmas in New York brought me face to face with another thing. My English mother had brought with her from the Old Country the English plum pudding made of suet, Zante currants, citron, and candied orange peel steamed in a bag. I viewed the New York variety with aversion and I still do. Years later a plum pudding of the old style came my way and I hailed it with delight. Fortunately for me in this strange new world mince pie was still mince pie.

CHAPTER II

First Steps in New York

M Y VENTURE in the big city was at best fumbling and uncertain. My assurance of a job on *McClure's Magazine* had little resemblance to a promise, largely because I had little to give. To be sure I had talked to Mr. McClure, but he had declined to give me any idea of the work I might be expected to do or the pay I might receive. That was entirely reasonable; what could I possibly do? He had made his own way all his life. All I had a right to expect was a chance to make good. As to pay, I was to discover soon that in my pay envelope was the same amount that my landlady charged for room and board. The outlook for early affluence was bleak.

To still further confound my confusion, in the summer before my senior year in college I had encountered the holder of a fellowship in the Columbia graduate school. He was attractive and seemed to think I might have the makings of a graduate student. So there I was shifting from foot to foot. I found the McClure office unorganized and tumultuous, and I seemed less important than the youngest office boy, so my mind turned back to the graduate school possibility. Perhaps I might feel more at home on Morningside Heights. I had been a considerable personage in college. Might not graduate school give me an echo of those glamorous days? So I became a student again.

I stuck to graduate school for three years, majoring in a combination of history and economics. Now I was on my own and I made my way by tutoring, free lance writing, a clerical post in the university, and a lucky prize or two, ending with money in the bank, but in general I found graduate school boring and meaningless. In prep school and college I had known three or four great teachers, people who seemed to care what happened to me. In graduate school I found only one, Franklin Giddings, a pioneer in sociology. He had begun as a newspaper writer and had derived much of the raw material of his lectures from that experience. His lectures were informal affairs in which students were expected to join. Most of the other faculty members seemed to view students as an interference with books that were being written or lectures being planned. One of them, a distinguished authority on constitutional law, read his lectures in one course from the manuscript of a book that he had published several years earlier. He began his course on comparative constitutional law by declaring that he admitted no women to his classes because of their obvious unfitness for dealing with such tough material. He confined his course to a detailed consideration of three governments, Germany, Great Britain, and the United States and of the three gave it as his considered opinion that the German was most likely to endure. It was his misfortune to live long enough to see Germany collapse in the bloody welter of the first world war.

For various reasons I felt myself on a dead-end street, and I determined to get out, hoping that my time in graduate school had not been entirely wasted. My intermittent writing had shown me that free lance writing will bring occasional jam, but for the daily bread a regular pay day is highly advisable and I landed a job on a weekly paper, *Public Opinion*. Here I found myself dealing with such matters as science, religion, art, literature, now and again foreign affairs, with book reviews for nights and Sundays. *Public Opinion* has long since gone the way of most of the magazines of that revolutionary period and the manner of its going is eloquent of the turbulent changes of the time. It was sold to the *Literary Digest*, our powerful competitor. Known then as the *Digest* and proud of its sucess as an election forecaster, it rashly foretold a landslide for Alfred Landon in 1936. When the slide boiled down to the states of Maine and Vermont, the *Review of Reviews* picked up the pieces of the *Digest*.

While my job on *Public Opinion* lasted, I found myself going through such a daily drill in the reporting and interpreting of important news as a graduate school had never afforded in anything. Our staff was small and we worked in close association in our study of the press of the world, domestic and foreign, from which we drew our material. In common with everybody else, we scrambled desperately for information and pictures when Mont Pelée on the Island of Martinique blew up and the city of St. Pierre with its thirty eight thousand inhabitants died in a fiery blast that left only one survivor in the deepest, darkest dungeon of a stone jail. The event is recalled as a time of frantic searching in the dark. We knew only that a great disaster had occurred and that the island where Empress Josephine had been born was somehow involved. Even the lordly New York *Herald* with its farflung network of "stand-by correspondents was as helpless as the rest of us. The men who might have told us the shocking news had died with the others in that instant of searing death.

That was a time when great disasters clamored in close succession for front page space. The flood that wrecked the city of Galveston, Texas in 1900, killed five thousand, but it is to be remembered for more than its list of dead. The city government was powerless to deal with the pressing problems of relief and rehabilitation and a group of leading citizens formed themselves into a temporary governing body. Out of this extemporized government emerged a permanent plan that spread rapidly to other cities struggling with corrupt political machines and irresponsible bosses, and city management became a recognized profession. A possible cure had been found for the ills that beset our cities. The people who died at Galveston had not died in vain.

Few disasters of that time brought such beneficent results. Most of them underlined official shortcomings and criminal neglect of one sort or another. A fire in the Iroquois Theater in Chicago killed nearly six hundred spectators, mostly women and children. The day after the fire, the Chicago *Tribune* summed it up in a banner headline, GOD DAMN THE CITY OF CHICAGO! New York had its share of murderous neglect and greed. A fire in a shirtwaist factory on Washington Place found emergency exits blocked with machinery and bales of inflammable material and women jumped from twelfth story windows to escape the flames. The *General Slocum*, a rickety old sidewheeler overloaded with women and children bound up the East River for a picnic, caught fire and more hundreds died. It was the same story of lax inspection and shameless greed.

My work on *Public Opinion* was absorbing and stimulating, dovetailing neatly into free lancing which I continued, presently venturing into the writing of books, four of them in less than ten years. The first one was a novel which somehow achieved publication. All that I remember of it now is that the last royalty statement showed, "No copies sold, one returned." When sales started running backward it seemed a good time to get off and I wrote no more novels, but I kept on writing books. The inner secret of such double duty is the discovery that there are twenty-four hours in a day; and so evenings, Sundays, and holidays found me at my typewriter putting words on paper to the elimination of my already slight social life. The fourth book of that period was my toughest assignment. An ambitious young publisher commissioned me to write a life of Lincoln for high school students, and I signed a contract to deliver the finished manuscript 90 days from the date of signing. Fortunately, I had read Anthony Trollope's autobiography and I took a leaf from the Trollope experience. The total number of words divided by the number of days gave me my daily ration of words on paper. I delivered the manuscript a week before it was due. Early sales of the book were promising, but the unfortunate death of the publisher put an end to that.

New York was a bonanza for the freelance writer around the

turn of the century. There were more than twice as many newspapers as there are today and new magazines were a matter of course. Of the lot, three names call for special attention: John Brisben Walker, Frank A. Munsey, and S. S. McClure. Walker may well have been the pioneer of the low-priced magazines of that revolutionary time. He was a restless, changeable, unpredictable character constantly embarking on new enterprises. At one time he was a cadet at West Point, resigning to become military adviser to the American minister in China to aid in the reorganization of the Chinese army. Later he became a manufacturer of steel in Western Pennsylvania, losing a tidy fortune in the panic years of the seventies. He was a sedulous writer for newspapers with a vague concern in social questions and advocated the development of the automobile as an aid in the improvement of highways.

In 1889 he bought the bankrupt *Cosmopolitan* and in five years raised the circulation from 16,000 to 400,000. In the same year he established the Cosmopolitan University, a low cost correspondence school. He was hard to understand and harder still to work for.

It was a lucky turn in Denver real estate that gave him working capital and he erected an impressive Greco-Roman temple on a high hill in Tarrytown, N.Y. Weird tales of his exploits began to be told about town. Once he decided that an entire issue of his magazine should be devoted to the Pan American exposition in Buffalo. Professing impatience with the slow fumbling process of ordinary writers, he descended upon the Buffalo scene and walked through the various exhibits with a stenographer at his elbow dictating his impressions as he walked. Walker wrote the entire issue, incidentally signing each separate chapter with his own name that there might be no mistaking the name of the doer of this fantastic job. There was soon a procession of editors and writers through the halls of his temple on the hill. A story was told among newspapermen of a newspaper artist who was offered the post of art editor on the growing *Cosmopolitan*. His colleagues

on the paper threw a banquet to celebrate their friend's escape
from the slavery and uncertainty of a daily paper. Then the fortunate young man took the train to Tarrytown to assume his new
dignities. As he paused on the platform to look about, a train was
just pulling out on the opposite track. As it began to move, a man
appeared running madly down the hill to catch the rear steps of
the last car where he stood a moment shaking his fist at the hill-
top temple. The new arrival asked an attendant standing near
who that character was and the reason for the menacing fist, to
be told that was the retiring art editor of the *Cosmopolitan* speaking his mind about his late employer and all his works. Presumably the new man soon went the same way. The *Cosmopolitan*
is now a part of the shrinking Hearst magazine empire.

The career of Frank Munsey was much simpler than that
of Walker. Born on a farm in Maine, he became a telegraph
operator in Augusta, then fertile soil for mail order publishing.
Young Munsey tried his hand at writing and achieved a book or
two on the Horatio Alger model. In 1888 he arrived in New York
with a bundle of manuscripts and forty dollars. Soon he concluded that publishing brought more returns than writing and his
course was determined. He was a lone wolf without partners and
only a nominal board of directors. He never married and had only
a casual social life. His ambition was simple, to make money.
When he died in 1926 his fortune was appraised at $19,747,687.
The bulk of this fortune he left to the Metropolitan Museum of
Art, even though he had shown little interest in art or in visiting
the institution.

Of him it may be said that he knew what he wanted and went
after it with all he had. Newspapers were added to magazines,
but he soon wearied of continual failure in this venture and
dropped his papers by the wayside. A chain of grocery stores, the
Mohican stores, was a money-maker as was the Munsey Trust
Company in Washington. His office was run as much as possible like a factory, no shirtsleeves and no smoking. Once he
lapsed into Maine vernacular and spoke of his "help," to the

annoyance of the intellectuals on his staff. When he died William Allen White wrote in the Emporia *Gazette* that he had the morals of a money changer and the manner of an undertaker.

It chanced that the ebb and flow of publications and publishers brought me to the Munsey staff for two separate terms, and gained for me the rank of "Live Wire," the Chief's equivalent of the Navy's "Well Done" — sometimes an uncomfortable category. There was the time he came up with the idea of an appraisal of United States Steel properties, lock, stock and barrel, and I was picked to do the job. He was a large holder of steel common and apparently didn't like the allegation that it was mostly water. His reasons were nothing to me, and for a few days I suffered the torments of the damned. What did I know about the value of a steel plant? I had never even walked through one and I knew nothing about the sinuosities of corporate accounting. Fortunately Judge Gary, chairman of the board of U. S. Steel got me off the hook. They knew the value of their properties, he said, and were in no need of amateur assistance or advice.

As a chapter in my book of experience, my few years on a magazine assembly line were interesting enough, although I view them now with incredulity. The total list of magazines that we turned out was overwhelming: *Munsey's, Argosy, All Story, Scrap Book, Railroad Man's Magazine* (my particular pigeon), *Ocean, Woman, Cavalier,* eight in all and I may have missed one or two. Their main difference was the name on the front cover.

Chief of all except the *Munsey* and the *Argosy* was Bob Davis. Born in Virginia City, Nevada, in the lush days of the Comstock Lode, he had gone through the hard school of the Hearst organization with a turn as Sunday editor of the *New York World.* Bob was a mixture of office tyrant, humorist, and raconteur without a peer. Most of the time my relations with him were harmonious, varied by brief bursts of unreasoning temper, and I owe him only gratitude for considerable additions to my education.

It was my hard lot later to witness a strange phrase in the career of Frank Munsey. For whatever reason, or no reason at all, he conceived it his duty to bring about a reduction in the number of New York papers. Having tried his hand unsuccessfully at launching new papers, he suddenly appeared as the angel of death to those already existing, and in due course announced the purchase or merger of papers of long standing reputation. In a year or two, he eliminated many of them such as the old morning *Sun*, famous as the newspaperman's newspaper and probably the expression of the most distinguished writing we have ever had with such men as Frank O'Malley, Bill Irwin, Al Thomas. The evening *Sun* lingered on in the Munsey garage eventually being absorbed by the Scripps-Howard *World-Telegram*, itself an amalgam of newspapers that had been. By the same route went the *Globe*, once the *Commercial Advertiser*, in my time a liberal organ and supporter of good causes, the friendly *Press*, my most dependable market, and the old conservative *Mail and Express*.

It was characteristic of this selfmade newspaper god that never by word or act did he express any interest in the fate of scores of good newspapermen that he turned loose to walk the streets looking for work. In that primitive day there was no Newspaper Guild to compel the granting of severance pay to these waifs of the storm. One case came close to the desk at which I was sitting in the Munsey building. Munsey had bought the infirm old *Herald* from the executors of the Bennett estate and was carrying it on with every appearance of continuance, at least no hint to the poor slaves of the paper. Then it was sold on three days notice to the *Tribune* to become the present *Herald-Tribune*. It is to the everlasting credit of the *Tribune* that it made every effort to take over as many as possible of the staff, even continuing the others on the payroll to give them a chance to find new jobs.

Probably there were too many papers competing for advertising and newsstand sales. Probably the present situation is more healthy, although that is a moot question. This observer has no inherent right to sit in judgment except for a strong belief that the

Munsey method was heartless and senseless. This was free enterprise — free and irresponsible.

In the hurly burly of newspapers and magazines, with writers coming and going, *McClure's* led the pack, and it was natural that my uncertain feet should lead me there in my first attempt to earn my own living. S. S. McClure, Sam to his close associates, had graduated from the same college as I, Knox, sixteen years earlier and was now a trustee of the college and a figure of importance in our small college world. There was about his success an aura of magic, of miracle working. How else could he have come so far in so short a time?

It would be difficult to find two men of the same period engaged in the same occupation and yet totally dissimilar as McClure and Munsey. For McClure his early struggles and privations were an important part of his saga. To Munsey early hardships and expedients were things to be ignored as though they were somehow shameful. Any reference to such experiences were resented coldly or denied.

Sam was born in the north of Ireland of that sturdy Scotch-Irish stock that has made such impressive contributions to our American civilization. After the death of his father, his mother had brought her four sons to America to find a home in Indiana near relatives of an earlier migration. An American cousin told Sam of Knox and urged him to go there and try working his way through. On his visit to the college, he loved to tell of his experiences in those hard days, living in a tent, taking to the road as a peddler when his scanty store of money ran close to the vanishing point, summers as a field hand or an itinerant worker at whatever kind of job he could find. The manner of his arrival at the college was a case in point. When he left Chicago on the last lap of his journey, he discovered that his cash would cover only a hundred and fifty miles of the hundred and sixty-three that lay before him and he finished his journey as a free rider. By whatever chance, luck, a crowded train, an absent-minded or benevolent conductor, he made it.

His resourcefulness was amazing. Induced by his mother to go with her on a swift trip to their old home in Ireland, he found himself without money for the return voyage. Not in the least disturbed, he pestered the first officer of a liner about to clear for America until that functionary gave him a job as helper in the ship's galley. The Irish lad nursed his nameless task into a post as pie-maker, sometimes turning out fifty pies in a single day. Out of that experience came the conviction that pie-making was a high art of which he was a master. Years later, on one of his frequent trips to Europe, he made boast of his old skill and his fellow passengers challenged him to a demonstration. The pies that resulted were raffled off to the considerable benefit of the seamen's fund of the ship.

In college he found himself confronted with Latin and Greek as requirements for the coveted A.B. He promptly fell in love with the classics, and soon developed a tremendous respect for the English insistence on familiarity with the traditional academic disciplines. To him here was the reason for the imperial greatness of Britain which became a fixed tenet of his faith. He also fell in love with the daughter of one of the professors, much to the latter's annoyance. It was the beginning of an engagement that was to last seven years until the father's objection to this penniless student as son-in-law finally changed to admiration and respect.

He found his first library at Knox — seven thousand volumes — and set himself to read them all as they stood in order on the shelves. He soon discovered that this method gave him little more than an indiscriminate mass of words, but he did find time to make a catalogue of the titles. It is a familiar story in American college annals, but to Sam it was a historic drama. It was at Knox that the idea that was to be a magazine began to take form. Two of his classmates were John S. Phillips and Albert Bird Brady, destined to be his associates in the founding of *McClure's*. These were singular chances that became part of his saga: to find a wife and two valuable associates on the way to a diploma was an unusual achievement in any college!

After college there was a brief period of groping, helping to edit and publish a house organ for the Columbia Bicycle Company — Sam was wont to refer to that as teaching people to do something he himself was unable to do — then a short turn on the *Century Magazine*, but the big adventure began to take form with the launching of the McClure Newspaper Syndicate. In essence, the plan of operation of the syndicate was simple in the extreme, nothing more than acting as intermediary between writers and newspapers. A single newspaper could hardly pay enough to keep the writer alive, but a group of papers could produce a respectable total for the writer and a reasonable commission for the syndicate. Now began a long acquaintance with a list of writers, many of them previously unknown to American readers, who were to provide the headlines for the magazine that was soon to be.

Americans knew magazines, or thought they did. There were many of them, *Harper's*, *Century*, *Scribner's*, the *Atlantic*, the *North American Review*, the *Forum*, the *Arena*, all very scholarly, dignified, and expensive. Many of them, *Harper's* for example, refused to consider the work of unknown writers. The editors sat in Olympian solitude communing with their consciences and burning incense to the great Brahmins of New England, most of whom were dead. The time was ripe for the men who would adventure with new names and new ideas. McClure knew some of the men. His syndicate had brought him in touch with them: Rudyard Kipling to whom Harper had turned an extremely chilly shoulder (pirating some of his stories later), Robert Louis Stevenson, Robert Barr, Conan Doyle, (the creator of Sherlock Holmes). McClure knew them all; if he didn't, he soon scraped acquaintance with them. If they were unknown, it would be his business to make them known

While the newspaper syndicate had provided the hopeful founders of the new enterprise with a list of possible contributors, they had no other capital and no sources from which they could

draw. Hope and a few names, these must serve as working capital. The amazing fertility of McClure's mind must not be over-
looked. Every morning was a new day with a dozen or more new
ideas. The only problem was to sort them out, separate the wheat
from the chaff. That was where John Phillips was invaluable.
His critical judgment was sound. S.S. proposed to roam about
looking for people and ideas. An important part of his plan was
that the new magazine was to be edited in the field, on the run
as it were. The old way led to imitation, repetition, stagnation.

The editor he visualized was to get out in the open, find
out what people were talking about, observe what they were
doing, ask questions, if possible find among them people who
were able and willing to write, set them to work and go on to the
next place. The mission of the new magazine was to hold a mirror
up to contemporary humanity so that reader might see themselves and the things they were doing. If this spelled education
and reform so much the better, but that must be incidental to the
main purpose. It was a big idea, but a vague one by the older
standards of editorial function.

To make the task harder, the year chosen for launching this
ambitious project, 1893, was a year of panic and disaster. Banks
closed, factories drew their fires, mines were shut down, bread
lines began to form on city streets, idle workmen stood in line
for a bowl of soup or a slice of bread flavored with meat. To
attempt something as radically new as the magazine they planned
took more than courage; it was a form of insanity. Nevertheless,
the three of them, McClure, Phillips, and Brady, turned to their
respective problems.

In the hard years ahead, Phillips was to prove again and
again his soundness and stability in their shaking world. He
brought to his work an understanding of the power and the beauty
of the written word. His taste was sure, his judgment immutable,
his critical sense accurate. He, too, was without magazine experience, but more than the others he knew the course that the new
magazine must steer. He followed the ups and downs of circula-

tion and the slowly rising tide of advertising. Afterwards he liked to tell of a time when S.S. barged in on him to ask, "John, do you know how much we owe?" John knew of course, just over a quarter of a million dollars owed to the printer, the paper maker, contributors, everybody in sight. S.S. thumped his knee with delight "Think of me being able to owe a quarter of a million dollars!" He had once spoken of himself as merely an Irish peasant with imagination; now he was a capitalist in reverse. The thought brightened the day for S.S., but not for John.

The part that Brady was to play, the third man in this singular trip, was as the seller of advertising space in the magazine. He, too, was a pioneer. The older magazines carried advertising, but a little grudgingly. Of course manufacturers must announce their wares, but it was not good form to do it blatantly or at high cost. The older magazines drew their chief income from subscriptions and the sale of single copies. That was the genteel thing to do; let advertising take care of itself. It was part of the McClure plan to reach as many readers as possible with this magazine edited for their benefit and hence to be offered at as low a price as possible. Fifteen cents a copy at the start soon reduced to ten. The sale of advertising space must fill the gap in the bill of costs. Brady wasted no time on explanation or apology; his job was to sell space and he went to it. The advertising pages were to be the market place of the world, and he made them so. Unfortunately he did not live to see the full fruition of his dream or its too early fading away.

Chapter III

Ida Tarbell

A NEW and valuable feature of the McClure plan was the practice of paying the writers of articles in proportion to the amount of time and effort in terms of research, travel, and interview rather than according to the number of words in the finished product. This inevitably resulted in the building up of a staff of experts. It became a part of the duty of the tireless McClure to find recruits for the staff and set them to work. One of the best he found was a woman, Ida Minerva Tarbell, destined to become one of the best known women in America. A chronicle of that time that lacks a chapter devoted to Miss Tarbell is incomplete.

She was born in the burgeoning oil country of northwestern Pennsylvania, Titusville, where new wells were being brought in almost daily and the air was filled with stories of riches beyond belief. Out of that place and time came a character calling himself "Coal Oil Johnny," somewhat more real than a similar specimen much later in Death Valley, California, who was known as "Death Valley Scotty." Johnny ran the usual gamut of private cars, parties for glamorous chorus girls, ten dollar tips for coatroom attendants, then he gave place to the solid men who were more interested in making money and keeping it than in throwing it away. One of the most solid was a young man named Henry H. Rogers lately come from Fairhaven, Mass., next door to New Bedford, once the home port of whalers who roamed the seven seas in their hunt for another kind of oil. Young Rogers was making his start with a small refinery and was almost a near neighbor of the Tarbells. He will appear later in this chronicle.

Miss Tarbell's father was a builder of oil tanks and distilling machinery and the young Ida was sent to Allegheny College at Meadville not far away. That was the time when coeducation was, in the minds of many, a dubious experiment; she was the only girl in her freshman class and certain of the campus walks were out of bounds for women. Miss Tarbell's vivid account of this period in her autobiography "All in the Day's Work" is illustrative of the early struggles of a small college in those formative years.

After college she turned automatically to teaching, there being little else available for educated women just out of college, and considered herself lucky to find an opening in the Poland Union Seminary in Ohio, five hundred dollars a year and "board yourself." For that magnificent sum she was expected to teach two classes in each of four languages, Greek, Latin, French, and German, plus classes in geology, botany, geometry, and trigonometry. On top of all this she learned after her arrival at the school that she was also responsible for two other subjects called respectively "verb grammar" and "percentage arithmetic" designed for the district school teachers of the region as prerequisites for promotion. Her impressive title was Preceptress and she endured this schedule for two years.

Then followed a period of resting and looking about for something else to try. This woman's life was to be a long series of experiments in doing things for which she had little prepation. Her first step after Poland Union Seminary was something of an accident but an important one; a short turn as assistant to the editor of the *Chautauquan*, a magazine published in connection with the work of the assembly directed by Dr. John H. Vincent. This was one of the striking institutions of the eighties, a combination of camp meeting, summer school, social center, and summer recreation area, fully equipped with assembly and study quarters, cabins, tent sites, bathing beaches, play grounds, and picnic spots, not to be confused with the Chautauqua circuit, a later development with which Miss Tarbell was to have some experience.

The original Chautauqua on Chautauqua Lake, N.Y., was founded in 1874 as a focal point for home study designed for the benefit of older people who had never had the opportunity for advanced study. It grew rapidly, but without losing its earlier characteristics, remaining essentially a summer school for all the picnic and holiday coloration it acquired. It was rooted in vacation territory, lakes, woods, hills, trees, and as replicas appeared in other states, Ohio, Indiana, as far away as Oregon they followed suit by seeking out a similar environment. The term lengthened from a few days or a fortnight to two months, with much of the phraseology and routine of a college, required courses, grades, examinations, diplomas, even colors and slogans. There was a Chautauqua salute: the waving of handkerchiefs.

Early in the century, 1903 perhaps, came the other Chautauqua, a weird combination of lectures, concerts, revivals, with a dash of vaudeville. Where the older institution had sought the open air and restful scenery the newcomer nestled in as close as possible to Main Street. Instead of two months the usual term was one week. Instead of permanent pavilions circus tents sheltered the crowds of spectators. The listeners were serious enough and there was little of the festival air of the circus, but the external look of things was reminiscent of Barnum & Bailey.

Back of this impressive array of program and feature was a hard tight organization of salesmen, advance men, and deceptively persuasive contracts. The technique was really simple. In every town seeking to be blessed with an installation, advance men engineered a local committee to sponsor the affair. This local sponsorship was the secret of the whole maneuver. These men, always local leaders with sound credit and money in the bank, were the guarantors who were to stand behind the enterprise, individually liable for the bills in the event of a washout. The salesmen reassured these worthies that they had only to sell a few season tickets, a paltry eight hundred or so at two fifty a throw, to put it over. The circuit managers also provided the performers, whether speakers, musicians, magicians, actors, Swiss bell ringers, acrobats. Of course circuit schedules were carefully dovetailed to prevent overlapping of dates and to provide the featured attraction with a long — and exhausting — season.

From the start the movement prospered until it began to spill over into Canada and even to have a try at Australia. The peak year was 1924 when it was estimated that 35,000,000 men, women and children sweated out summer afternoons under the huge tents. Then the movement collapsed as though a vein of precious metal had been worked out; the peak year was also the last, but it was an amazing spectacle while it lasted.

To those of us immersed in our own concerns in the big cities, these tented revivals or circuses or whatever else they were at various times and places were vaguely amusing manifestations of rural high jinks. We occasionally looked on with vague mild wonder, but they were not for us. We were not among the 35,-000,000 of the last great year, but as viewed in the long perspective of nearly half a century a few things begin to come clear in this curious phenomenon. There was that vague hunger for something that might be called culture. Eugene Field once remarked that when Chicago got around to culture, "she'd make it hum!" Chautauqua was doing that on a large scale. Another item appears—we were strong for moral uplift. Our specifications were few and simple, work hard, pay your debts, go to church regularly send your children to school, live decent simple lives. We were not a nation of philosophers although Emerson had been a popular lecturer in the days of the old Lyceum.

The stars of the tent Chautauqua were significant. William Jennings Bryan was made to order as a trouper. He had enormous vitality, he could sleep anywhere, he could travel on anything, he could eat large quantities of plain food, and the Midwest had plenty of that and he had a voice that could dominate the largest crowd. His "Prince of Peace" was sure fire with two thousand appearances on the record. He was Chautauqua while he lasted. Another sterling performer was Russell H. Conwell with his one subject "Acres of Diamonds," over six thousand renditions. Out of his profits from this act he founded a university, Temple University in Philadelpha, present enrollment around 20,000. The theme of "Acres of Diamonds" was the importance of material success and the wide range of opportunities for worldly advancement. Bryan and Conwell were masters of the "inspirational appeal." What they said was of minor importance; the important thing was the "appeal."

There is no need at this late date to list the various features that the programs carried. If you had said or done or written something, almost anything, you were fair game for Chautauqua. One daring agent made a try for Mark Twain but that wily performer had had enough of the platform and the spotlight. Young Winston Churchill ran over to have a look but a New York taxi sent him to a hospital, probably a break for Winston. Editors, war correspondents, novelists, actors, candidates for office, Chautauqa raked them in, put them through the mill, kept them for a repeat or dropped them by the wayside. LaFollette of Wisconsin came and told about his Progressive movement, but not very happily. The Chautauqua schedule was too hard and inflexible for him, he was by nature a lone operator. Steffanson of the Arctic gave it a whirl but he found the hurly burly of talent under the big top confusing and poorer company than his Eskimo friends in the frozen North. Generally speaking only the veterans, the gypsies of the tank towns and the one night stands, had the necessary endurance and adaptability. Bryan and Conwell were exceptions any way one took them.

Why did Chautauqua collapse so suddenly on the heels of its biggest year? Probably the reasons were various, available talent of the top drawer variety was scarce and the vaudeville features grew more and more pronounced. The tight contract that bound the local committee in full responsibility began to chafe and potential sponsors shied away. The powerful contract which had lifted Chautauqua to the peak became the means of its downfall. The vein was worked out.

For all the flamboyance of the tented Chautauquas and their sudden demise the original institution on the shores of Lake Chautauqua was holding fast to its original course of summer study with special textbooks and manuals of study and examinations. What was particularly to the point, was providing young Ida Tarbell, two years out of college, with useful training for a future career. On the staff of the *Chautauquan* she was having her first experience in research for the editing or writing of articles, although time and sources of material were limited. Her thoughts were turning back to an old dream, foreign travel and advanced study, preferably in Paris, and in 1891 with three other ambitious young women she sailed for France to gamble her small savings, supplemented by the sale of articles to American newspapers and magazines on various aspects of life in Paris which she hoped to write. There were many days when the going was hard and the nest egg dangerously shrunken, but she stuck it out for two wonderful years

Then one day there was a knock on the door of their small apartment and a slender little man appeared to introduce himself as S. S. McClure, head of the McClure Newspaper Syndicate to which she had sold a few articles. This was destiny in human form. Although he had announced that he could stay only fifteen minutes he stretched his time to nearly three hours and after he left Miss Tarbell realized to her own amazement that she had agreed to do a life of Napoleon for a new magazine that was about to start. She realized that she had loaned forty dollars to her visitor to carry him on to his next appointment in Geneva. The new magazine of course was McClure's and in 1894 she was back in New York hard at work on her assignment. She did her Napoleon chiefly in the form of expanded captions for a series of portraits of the conqueror. Then it was Abraham Lincoln as he was remembered by men still living. That too was a McClure idea.

Soon after Lincoln's death his two secretaries, John G. Nicolay and John Hay, had begun work on an authoritative life of the Emancipator, a ten-volume affair of the Life and Times order. Miss Tarbell sought out Nicolay in Washington for advice on source of new material. Nicolay froze at once; probably exploded would be a better word. New material indeed! There was no such thing. He and Hay had told all there was to tell about Lincoln. He told this young upstart that she was trespassing on his private domain. Even after publication of Miss Tarbell's Lincoln began he called on her to make a final protest. "You are invading my field. You write a popular life of Lincoln and you do just so much to reduce the value of my property." Lincoln belonged to him by right of prior settlement! Incredible but true.

The most important as well as most controversial of Miss Tarbell's many achievements was her history of the Standard Oil Company. So many rumors and baseless assertions have clustered around this work that it may help to tell the story as it was told to me by Miss Tarbell and John Phillips long after the tumult and the shouting had died down. One of the most insistent versions was that she was actuated by a desire for revenge for wrongs done to her father by Standard Oil. Another yarn purported to give the details of attempts to destroy the standing of the magazine with banks and advertisers.

The story of avenging the wrongs done to her father is sheer nonsense, although some historians have accepted it as gospel. The elder Tarbell was not a driller or refiner but a manufacturer of tanks and refining machinery and not a competitor with Standard. So there were no wrongs to avenge, nor was any attempt made to destroy the credit standing of the magazine. John Phillips put it succinctly: "The Standard Oil articles increased our circulation and advertising and improved our credit. They put us on our feet."

It was the original plan of the staff to publish a series of articles celebrating the achievements of American business and Standard Oil was chosen to head the list as the largest and most sensational of them all. Miss Tarbell later stated the case in her auto-biography: " '*McClure's* has courage.' How often that remark was made after our undertaking was underway. But courage implies a suspicion of danger. Nobody thought of such a thing in our office. We were undertaking what we regarded as a piece of historical work. We were neither apologists nor critics, only journalists intent on discovering what went into the making of this most perfect of all monopolies. What had we to be afraid of?"

To complete the picture the material for the opening chapters was obtained from the active head of Standard Oil, Henry H. Rogers, who had begun his career in oil as a near neighbor of the Tarbells in Titusville. In due course John D. Rockefeller had spotted him as a valuable man for Standard and had transformed him from competitor to ally. I saw Mr. Rogers only once but I remember him as one of the handsomest men I ever saw. Slender, impeccably dressed, courtly in manner, he might well have been a Medicean prince in the great days of Renaissance Italy.

Mark Twain, a close friend of Rogers, acted as intermediary in introducing Miss Tarbell to him, and the first two or three chapters were written in close cooperation with Rogers who gave her access to the files and books of the corporation. He read the finished chapters in manuscript and offered comments and criticisms. The stage setting for these interviews, as described by Miss Tarbell, was interesting. The writer was admitted to the inner sanctum immediately on her appearance in his waiting room. When the session ended she was ushered out by another door into a different waiting room and shown the way to a different elevator, insuring a high degree of privacy.

Being a good reporter, Miss Tarbell was not content with this official version of corporate growth and power but began investigations of her own, newspaper reports of trials, legislative hearings, any reports available on the growing mass of evidence, rumors, charges, denials that inevitably clustered around the career of the largest trust yet to appear and she did not fail to note a singular tendency on the part of rival refineries to burn down or to suffer other catastrophes that did not seem to happen to Standard. These things began to be woven into the articles and of course came to Mr. Rogers' attention. She told me of the day when he mentioned the results of her digging. She was greeted with the usual courtesy and bowed to her chair, but this time Rogers held the manuscript in his hand and looked at her in quiet inquiry: "These burnings and explosions in other refineries, are they essential, Miss Tarbell?" The young woman naturally expected something like this and was ready with her counter question; "They happened, didn't they, Mr. Rogers?" Without a change in his courteous manner, he said, "Yes, I suppose they did." A pause then, "Those were rough times, Miss Tarbell, and rough things were done." That was all. No threats, not even a raising of the quiet voice. He returned the chapter to its author with the usual bow and the words: "I fear I shall not be able to be of further service to you in your work." That was the sum total of truth in the mass of rumors of corporate threats, pressure on banks and advertisers and all the rest of the inventions, guesses, and plain lies. There was only this quiet drama in the sanctum at 26 Broadway.

The Standard Oil series brought prosperity to the magazine and that in turn brought dissension to the staff. It may be that the rapid growth had gone to the McClure head. The magazine was just out of its first decade but its influence was wide. Editorials praised it for its enterprise and courage, ministers commented from their pulpits on its power as an engine of social uplift and a leader in civic betterment. Ever since the magazine had demonstrated its ability to stand on its own feet S.S. had urged his associates to join the launching of a McClure weekly, but the staff failed to take fire at the idea.

Oppositon only stimulated S.S. in the making of larger plans, a universal magazine that should do for the world what *McClure's* was doing for the United States, a colossal savings bank, an insurance company, a housing development, all to bear the name of the miracle working McClure. There appeared to be no limit to the dreams of this unpredictable genius for whom the world was made over fresh every morning. There was long sparring, many consultation and proposals. The staff that had been so united and eager through the years of struggling growth began to break apart and the McClure-Phillips combination ceased to exist. Most of the key people stood with Phillips, Miss Tarbell, Steffens, Baker, Bert Boyden, whom I had known in the old Knox Academy, now an able managing editor. The choice offered to McClure was to buy or sell and his first impulse was to sell his interest to the dissenters, but a night's sleep revealed to him that if he sold he would have no magazine to be the core of his new ventures and it was the opposition who sold.

In retrospect it is clear that this was the first fading of a great vision. *McClure's* was to go on for several years under shifting management but only a fading shadow of its former greatness. Phillips had been the balance wheel, the governor to regulate the driving energy of McClure. Once he characterized his former associate as a "timid man," but without him S.S. was doomed to wander in a jungle of possibilities most of which remained without form. The staff that had given symmetry and form to the magazine was gone and their like was hard to find. Under the leadership of Phillips that staff stuck together to find a new home on the *American,* once *Frank Leslie's Popular Monthly.* Two new and important names appeared on the staff of the reconstructed *American,* William Allen White, editor of the Emporia, Kans., *Gazette,* and Finley Peter Dunne, the creator of "Mr. Dooley." Both men were products of that day when newspaper work was a training school for genius. White had bought the *Gazette* on the traditional shoe string and by hard work and a sure instinct for small town journalism had made of it a national organ. His editorial essay, "What's the matter with Kansas?" was copied by scores of papers in all parts of the country. Politically he was a Republican but a new model and he fought the shabby figures in his own party even harder than those on the other side. The *Gazette* circulation remained small

but it was powerful, making it the envy of newspapermen everywhere. He had written short fiction for *McClure's* and he was
proud to be a consultant on the staff of the new American.

Finley Peter Dunne became a working member of the staff
with a department of his own "The Interpreter's House." Dunne
had won his spurs on the old Chicago *Journal* when such men
as Eugene Field and George Ade were riding high in the newspaper firmament and the young Carl Sandburg was coming into
view. Dunne made his first great reputaton as the creater of "Mr.
Dooley." Dooley was supposed to be a saloonkeeper on the "Archy
Road" and Hennessey was his stooge on the other side of the bar,
the drinking not the working side. It was Hennessey's function to
ask the silly questions, make the foolish generalizations, and
otherwise act as "feeder" for the wise Dooley. Dunne had a keen
eye for the vulnerable points of the news and his understanding
of the political scene was deep. The published volumes of Mr.
Dooley's wit and wisdom should he required reading for students
of the history of that day.

There was no brogue in Dunne's department of the *American* but much wisdom and it often included contributions by other
members of the staff. Miss Tarbell in her autobiography ruefully
admits her own inability to measure up to the Interpreter's standard and quotes Dunne's laconic explanation, "Miss Tarbell, you
sputter like a woman." Perhaps, but a few sputters may be permitted to this woman who gave so much form and substance to
the writing of her time.

In her new environment Miss Tarbell turned her attention
to other aspects of business, the possibility of the Golden Rule
as part of the policy of industry, the improvement of housing for
workers, the position of women in industry, the increased use
of safety appliances. She wrote biographies of Owen D. Young,
the head of General Electric, and Judge Gary, chairman of the
board of U.S. Steel, whom she regarded as the Statesman of Industry; then a book analyzing the "Growth of Big Business." She
was a firm believer in women's rights, but not as Mrs. Carrie

Chapman Catt and Dr. Anna Shaw saw them. To Miss Tarbell the granting of the suffrage to women was an act of simple justice and her realistic mind refused to believe that the votes of women would work miracles of political righteousness. She toured the Chautauqua circuit and gave William J. Bryan much pain by refusing to agree on the road to peace; Bryan saw himself as much more than a feature of the program. He was the program, no one else counted. Miss Tarbell stood pat and spoke her mind as always. Touring the Chautauqua circuit was a strenuous experience even for this hard worker — forty-nine lectures on forty-nine successive days in forty-nine different places.

She might be regarded as the first of the "muckrakers," a name contributed by Theodore Roosevelt who lifted it from one of his favorite books of reference, "Pilgrim's Progress." The muckraker was the character who raked in the muck refusing to lift his eyes to the many beauties about him, incidentally one of the snappiest of T. R.'s many snap judgments. In sober reality writers like Miss Tarbell exposed not jewels but misdeeds; the term was a badge of honor. Whatever the merits of the case Ida Tarbell was not only a great woman, one of the greatest, she was also a great citizen.

CHAPTER IV

"Stef" and Some Others

A NOTHER active member of the staff of *McClure's* was Lincoln Steffens. Here was a different figure from the rank and file of magazine and newspaper writers. Born in California of a family of at least comfortable income, he was educated at the University of California in Berkeley. The study of philosophy interested him as did the causes and processes of revolution. Was there such a thing as a science of good government? From Berkeley his studies took him to Germany, Berlin, Leipsic, Heidelberg, finally Paris.

When it became necessary to return to the United States his first job was covering Wall Street for the *Commercial Advertiser*, soon to become the *Globe*. Then he was shifted to police headquarters where he became aware of the relationship of policemen with crooks. The shadow of Inspector Byrne was still heavy at headquarters and the use of stool pigeons was standard technique in police work. Was that one of the causes of bad government? He became city editor and continued his interest in the bizarre partnership of law enforcement with law breaking. He formed a friendship with Richard Croker, the head of Tammany Hall, and found him surprisingly helpful. Perhaps there was a larger problem here than he had thought in his student days.

Tammany Hall has been much criticized for its corrupt practices — and deservedly so, but there is another side to the shield. The "Hall" was also a definite force in social welfare. It was the business of a district leader to know the people of his district and to come to their aid in time of need. A roast turkey, a few bags of coal, a doctor and medicine for a sick child were tangible proof of the leader's good will. There were district clubs for the young men and these were active social centers of a neighborhood with amateur plays, minstrel shows, and debates that could create, in a shabby region, the atmosphere of a friendly village. Let these items be posted on the credit side of the Tammany Hall ledger.

Steffen's next break was a call from S. S. McClure; would he take the peripatetic editorship of the magazine? Here was his chance for a look at a larger field than police headquarters in New York. Now "Stef," as he was called among his fellows, began his investigations of the shabby side of city government which developed into the "Shame of the Cities." The choice of the city to head this malodorous list was wide open; he could hardly go wrong. As urban populations had multiplied the number and difficulty of the services required had increased and the ability of the old type of government to meet the demand had diminished. Irresponsible bosses had usurped the power supposed to rest in the hands of mayors and aldermen and in most urban centers machines instead of decent citizens took charge. In too many places, the men who should have been the leading figures of the community accepted the rule of the machine and the boss, often actively conniving in it. Businessmen found they could "do business" with vice and crime and actually profit by it. Wherever Steffens looked the answer was the same; big businessmen were too busy to bother with politics. They told themselves that the bosses got things done. You knew where you were with them.

Stef observed that things seemed to be happening in St. Louis where an energetic young prosecuting attorney named Folk was making trouble for politicians and crooks and he chose St. Louis for his first chapter of exposure. A reporter for a local paper was engaged to work with him and the chapter on St. Louis carried two signatures, one instance at least where the McClure plan of a wandering editor and a local writer seemed to work. S.S. was a genius of a sort with an extraordinary ability to walk into a situation and catch the essentials of it in a short time. There was where his plan broke down. He alone could make his own idea work. E. W. Scripps had a similar quality among newspaper workers, but he combined with it a willingness to delegate full authority which McClure could never quite bring himself to do.

Steffens made friends easily as he had shown in his dealings with Richard Croker in New York. He cultivated bosses and their henchmen and they talked to him with surprising frankness. He noted their contempt for the "goody-goody" element in politics as he also noted the tendency of the good to evade questions touching their own responsibility to the public interest. It was that way in St. Louis, San Francisco, Philadelphia, Minneapolis, and Chicago. Only in Cleveland and Toledo did he find a difference. He said of Cleveland that it was the best governed city in the United States. That was Tom Johnson's town.

Steffens was ill at ease in the new environment of the *American* — in his autobiography he explains that he found himself making too much money; another version has it that he complained he wasn't making enough. Whatever the reason he was clearly at a loss to adjust himself to the changed conditions and launched forth on an odd crusade, a search for a cure for the ills that afflicted mankind perhaps to be found in the places of storm and upheaval; so he set forth with notebook and pencil, a pilgrim in search of a plan and a gleam of hope in a dark sky.

With the breaking apart of the old McClure staff there began this new chapter in the Steffens saga, the most interesting and in many ways the most baffling of his crowded career. The air of that time was electric with ideas. Many men were seeking definitions and explanations for such things as Revolution, Liberty, Good Men and Bad Men and Stef sought out these men and talked with them. There was Tom Johnson of Cleveland. He was a baffler, jolly, laughing, sincere and rich. How did he get that way?

Johnson was born of a Southern family impoverished by the war and seems to have been endowed from birth with an instinct

for making money. He began early. The conductor on a train
running into Stanton, Virginia, gave him a tip on the profits to
be made selling papers to travelers and agreed to give him the
exclusive right to ride his train. It was a good thing while it
lasted which was until the friendly conductor was transferred to
another run. That taught the eleven-year old boy his first lesson
in the technique of money-making, look for the place where a
monopoly was to be had. That pointed straight at municipal traction. He tried his wings in Indianapolis, then shifted to Cleveland
and was a millionare before he was thirty.

He took no thought of politics except as he might use political influence for his own purposes. A chance remark by another
railroad conductor led him to read a book by Henry George,
"Social Problems." There he stumbled on a word he was never to
forget, Privilege. The men who made the big money and kept
it were those who were in a monopoly position. That led him to
a stretch of self-examination at the end of which he concluded
that he himself was a beneficiary of Privilege. There was the
basic difference between the rich and the poor. The son of a
poor man might fight his way to the top but he was never secure
except that he established a position of Privilege. That was where
the Rockefellers, the Vanderbilts, the Carnegies, and coming
nearer home Mark Hanna of Cleveland were entrenched.

He read George's *Progress and Poverty* and talked with
George in his Brooklyn home and began to understand the prin-
ciple of the Single Tax. Land was basic. The men who held the
land could not be beaten. Whatever happened they were secure.
Railroads, factories, cities, even trolley lines on city streets must
pay tribute to the owner of the land. The land owner could give
orders to legislators, mayors, judges, taxing bodies and they must
work his will. His was the last word, in banks, churches, schools,
and chambers of commerce. Young Johnson turned all this over
in his mind and the more he thought the more he was determined
to find a way out of his dilemma. Could the cure be as simple as
Henry George said it was? He challenged his friends, lawyers,

businessmen, tax experts, to find the flaw in George's reasoning and as he answered their questions and met their criticisms he argued himself into a complete acceptance of the George thesis.

He did not immediately throw overboard his traction interests but he reversed his attitude. Traction companies owned land and presumably served the public, most of them poor people, but the owners rigged the laws and the courts and the police, to avoid fair taxation and so increase their profits. Here was the perfect monopoly, the apotheosis of Privilege. That was where Johnson became the firm advocate of city owned low fare traction, three cent fares with unlimited transfers. Of course the respectable citizens, bankers, directors of corporations, even some minsters, denounced him as a Socialist, an anarchist. Men like Hanna might respect him in private, and most of them did, but in public he was a dangerous and insidious enemy.

In spite of bitter opposition Johnson began to find supporters, especially among working men who were the chief trolley riders and he was elected to Congress. National politics failed to appeal and he turned back to his adopted city Cleveland and continued to hammer home his basic argument, that was to bring back to the public the ownership of the land on which all other privilege rested. Recapture the land for the common good he declared and the other social ills will cure themselves. He once told Theodore Roosevelt that the real difference between the two of them was that T. R. wanted to punish law breakers while he, Johnson, sought to prevent law breaking.

He became mayor of Cleveland and held that office nine years. That was the time when Lincoln Steffens said of him that he was the best mayor of the best city in the United States. He infected younger men, Newton D. Baker, Fred Howe, Fred Kohler, (whom he made chief of police) and many others with his zeal for public service. He demanded of the men he appointed to city posts that they do their jobs to the best of their ability. He made the city of Cleveland a model of decency, honesty, and good government so that men who had been among his bitter critics, came over to his side and fought shoulder to shoulder with him. Steffens talked with him and his chief supporters and rendered his verdict, "Best mayor of the best city in the United States," but that was not what Stef was looking for. No graft or corrupt alliances here and the student of bad government went on his way. Fred Howe said of Johnson that he was the greatest statesman in the United States.

When he died in 1911 he believed that the Single Tax was on its way both here and overseas. Perhaps it was; we shall never know. Three years later the march of armies filled all ears and still does and the full testing of the Henry George theory is still on the list of unfinished business. But if he never saw the fulfillment of his dream Tom Johnson did see the beginning of better city government toward which he made large contributions.

In Toledo, Steffens talked with Samuel (Golden Rule) Jones, a successful businessman and a good mayor who claimed that it was possible to practice the Golden Rule in both business and politics. Jones too was a genial soul and read Walt Whitman and the New Testament to the inquiring reporter. In Denver Stef looked in on Judge Ben Lindsey and his childrens' court. Lindsey assured him that there were no such things as "good" boys and "bad" boys, there were only boys. It was environment that made the difference and the boys the police called troublemakers were usually the easiest to deal with if you went about it the right way because they were the most intelligent. In Chicago Steffens talked with Clarence Darrow, chronic counsel for the defense and foe of capital punishment. He laughed at Stef for believing there is such a thing as honesty. All these men agreed that the destruction of the poor is their poverty.

Word of disaster and violence affected Stef as the sound of a gong calls to an old fire horse. When a bomb exploded in the building of the Los Angeles *Times* killing twenty-one people and the McNamara brothers, prominent labor agitators, were arrested and charged with the crime Steffens hurried out to look into it.

His first intention was to join in the defense of the two brothers, then having convinced himself of their guilt he stayed on as a conciliator. In that capacity he worked out a plan for compromise and convinced Gen. Otis, chief owner of the *Times* and a staunch foe of labor unions, of its essential soundness. A scalp-hunting prosecuting attorney refused to cooperate and hope of a compromise vanished. It was a confused and confusing situation that not even Steffens was able to make clear in his autobiography.

After the McNamara fiasco Steffens wandered down into Mexico to look into the tangle of revolutions that had followed the flight of Porfirio Diaz who had ruled as a dictator for fifty years. Venustiano Carranza looked good to him; perhaps here was the herald of the dawn, but Carranza went the way of other Mexican aspirants, the killer's way. Disappointed in Mexico Stef thought he had found the proper herald in Benito Mussolini, the renegade Italian Socialist who made a black shirt a symbol of empire and the recapture of the ancient glories of Rome. Steffens in Italy was only one of many Americans who fell for this strutting, posturing adventurer. It was a strange thing to hear even level-headed Ida Tarbell praise him for making Italian trains run on time and for achieving the miracle of a long distance telephone call from Rome to Milan completed within the space of a single day.

This widespread bowing before cardboard saviors of mankind was like something out of Hollywood. My old professor of constitutional history in graduate school had awarded the palm to the German empire as the best government yet devised. That was bad enough, but at least the Kaiser had played his role to the limit. Why did so many sensible Americans ignore the plain teaching of their own history? We had withstood the strain of war, endured the rascalities of businessmen and crooked politicians and were still governing ourselves and not too badly. Was it possible that the searchers for a sure formula were looking for something that didn't exist, never had and never would? Our history as a people deserves careful, intelligent study. Most of the time we have plodded along, taking things as they came, building railroads, towns, mills, schools, and colleges, most of the time improving a little here and there as we learned a better way of managing our affairs, not always too brilliantly, paying our way, picking up the pieces, and with the exception of some of our windy Fourth of July orators, doing it all with commendable modesty.

All the way across the continent from Plymouth Rock to the Pacific we had been learning how to govern ourselves. Read the Mayflower Compact and observe the growth of the New England town meeting that Jefferson called "that precious kernel of democracy." Good government is not to be achieved by repeating a formula or pressing a button. It comes as a result of hard work by many kinds of people, good and less good, and it is not handed down from above. The biggest mistakes of the two great English-speaking people have been made when they let their minds go wandering off in search of glory and profit. Great Britain and the United States alike have need to ponder this profound truth. Good and Bad cannot be isolated in separate test tubes as though they were new chemicals.

Naturally this student of humanity in torment turned finally to Russia to find the secret sources of social justice. On the staff of *McClure's* he had been much taken with young Jack Reed, talented, confused, groping. Reed had landed in Petrograd in time to witness the arrival of Lenin, and his small book "Ten Days That Shook the World" is an extraordinary document in contemporary history. In Russia Stef was all too easily convinced that he had found the answer to all his questions. His verdict was succinct: "I have seen tomorrow and it works." His tomorrow is now our yesterday and his land of promise is only one more greedy, ruthless power. Meanwhile the two great English-speaking democracies are carrying on, building, changing, making mistakes and correcting some of them, and generally governing themselves.

The term "muckraker" has been much misused, and not by Theodore Roosevelt only. Many of the writers of that period were in reality demonstrating the self-correcting processes of democracy, throwing light in dark corners much as the freeholders of New England did in the town meetings. Critics of Ida Tarbell labelled her a mere sensational journalist skillfully skirting the edge of libel. Such a verdict is nonsense. She was a trained historian collecting evidence, checking and confirming and reporting what she found. The same could be said of Steffens in the "Shame of the Cities." In his later pilgrimages in Mexico, Italy, Russia, and elsewhere he was neither journalist or historian, perhaps a lone wanderer in a pathless wilderness.

Ray Stannard Baker was another useful member of the old McClure team and later of the *American*, totally different from Steffens and assuredly not a muckraker. He had been a top reporter for the old Chicago *Record* and had caught the eye of McClure by his writing for the syndicate and especially by an article for the magazine on the capture of John Wilkes Booth in which his grandfather had played a prominent part. Later he did a series of articles for the magazine which developed into a book "Following the Color Line," an objective treatment of race relations and a foreshadowing of things to come. He was also a close student of railroads and their financial difficulties. His work was always a solid factual dealing with observed reality with no striving for sensationalism.

On the *American* he showed another aspect of his interest by articles under the nom de plume of David Grayson. Not many people knew of this duality. As David Grayson he wrote quietly and humorously of the life of a small New England town, still tolerant, wise, thoughtful. Here was probably the man he would have chosen to be in another incarnation. His final status was at the official biographer of Woodrow Wilson, certainly not a muckraking task. Baker was the member of the old staff I knew first and in many ways best, gentle in manner, friendly, helpful, wise. He was the first New York editor to buy any of my stuff and also the first to turn any of it down, thereby giving further proof of his friendly wisdom.

The muckrake, if muckrake it was, was swung widely by

many men in many mediums. One of the best known of these varied workers was Samuel Hopkins Adams. He too began as a reporter, one of the best, trusted by editors and beloved by all his fellow reporters. His contribution to the literature of the time was made for *Collier's Weekly* in the form of a series of articles on the flourishing trade in proprietary medicines. The tycoons of the patent medicine world had been riding high, wide and handsome and were overdue for a fall. Adams knew there would be libel suits and he provided himself with affidavits by reliable chemists showing the exact ingredients of the widely advertised cures for cancer, consumption, any or all of the diseases that afflict mankind.

When the truth about these noisome brews became known there were screams of pain from the proprietors along with threats of suit, few of which were ever brought and none were won. The outcome of this thorough job of digging was a pure food and drugs act which required that the label on the bottle tell the whole truth about the contents. When Upton Sinclair's novel "The Jungle" with its sensational picture of conditions in the big packing-houses and of the quarters in which the workers lived appeared, it became clear that the charges of "embalmed beef" furnished to our troops in the Spanish-American war had sober confirmation and even Theodore Roosevelt, who had been prompt to slap the label muckraking on this type of article, was equally prompt to use the evidence that had been raked up. Harvey W. Wiley, the chief of the new bureau, saw to it that offenders felt the bite of the teeth that the law supplied.

Not all of this work of investigation and reform was as carefully done as was that of the reliable men and women who have been named. By this time William Randolph Hearst had acquired the *Cosmopolitan* that John Brisben Walker had developed and was making of it something vastly different from the rather stodgy affair that Walker had conceived. The new *Cosmopolitan* was quick to seize upon exposure as a circulation builder and a well known novelist David Graham Phillips went to work with a spotlight trained upon the United States Senate. There were vulnerable spots in the senate roll and it was fairly common knowledge that certain members of that august body represented interests, railroads, lumber, mines, cattle rather than people, but the charge of Treason could hardly be brought against the senate as a whole. The *Cosmopolitan* claimed too much and proved too little.

An echo of this frenzy of exposure reached me sitting uneasily at the editor's desk of unimportant *Public Opinion*. *Everybody's*, a newcomer among magazines, was publishing a series of articles by Thomas W. Lawson, speculator, broker, breeder of fancy cattle, one time owner of an unsuccessful aspirant for the defense of the America's Cup, and afflicted with an itch to get square for wrongs he claimed to have suffered at the hand of Thomas F. Ryan of New York. Those were the days when stock market operations were rough, tough, and uncontrolled. The Securities Exchange Commission was still far in the future. Lawson's series had the appropriate title of "Frenzied Finance."

One day word came down to me from high up in the vague category of *Public Opinion* ownership that we were to run a reply to Lawson to be entitled "The Truth About Lawson." Mine not to reason why or how. The writer of our screed had been selected and in due course copy began to come to me. I bowed my shaky head and shoved it along to the printer. Of course there were charges that we had sold out to the enemies of the man in Boston. One letter stated the amount, $20,000; none of that came my way. All that happened was a brief period of excitement and the threat of a criminal libel suit, not by Lawson himself but by an insignificant hanger-on who had been referred to as a "race track tout." The suit was never brought and poor old *Public Opinion* continued to slide gently in the direction of the scrap heap.

CHAPTER V

Carnegie Shows the Way

EVER since the Civil War, private fortunes had been growing in the victorious North especially in oil and steel and
the building and manipulation of railroads. Some of us regretted
and deplored, but more and more we pointed with pride and talked
of the day when our wealth would overtop that of the great British empire. In 1904 John Moody published a book "The Truth
About the Trusts," listing 318 industrial "trusts" with a dizzying
total capitalzation of more than seven billion dollars. The biggest
and most sensational of them all was United States Steel. This
was the brainchild of Andrew Carnegie, master of steel, who
was threatening to gather the world of steel into one huge
company. Other steel men shrieked with alarm and J. Pierpont
Morgan, master banker, brusque, imperious, irascible, proposed
that steel maker and banker sit down and talk things over. The outcome was the purchase of Carnegie's interests for $477,000,000,
payable in bonds and preferred stock. The resultant merger, to
be known as the United States Steel Company, had an estimated
value of $682,000,000 and the capitalization of the new combina-
tion was a tidy total of $1,402,847,000, bonds, preferred stock,
and common. All the common and a slice of the preferred was
"water" — faith in the future if you prefer. The news of this
affair that was genuinely sensational was Carnegie's idea, nothing
less than giving away his money. U. S. Steel is still with us and,
on the whole, in good health.

In his book "The Gospel of Wealth" Carnegie had enun-

ciated his belief that great wealth brought great responsibility, a stewardship in reality. His slogan was "The man
who dies rich dies disgraced." Large scale benefaction was
something new to Americans. To be sure Rockefeller had
been giving considerable aid to churches and schools, especially to the refounded University of Chicago, ($34,000,000
before 1904) but the university was in operation under highly
competent leadership — President Willam Rainey Harper was a
genius among college heads. As Carnegie's plan developed it
began to be evident that what he was considering was a group or
series of philanthropic corporations each with a field and function of its own.

Carnegie was born in Scotland in wretched circumstances
and had begun his American career as a telegraph operator during
the Civil War. Now he found himself in possession of apparently
unlimited power. His belief in the efficacy of money for the cure
of the world's ills was incredbly naive. His whole training had
been in the making of money and not in giving it away. No one
had yet learned that giving away money is far from simple or easy.
That knowledge was to come later under the direction of a younger Rockefeller. Much of Carnegie's benefaction was a groping
for purpose and program. His first tentative efforts were obvious, acknowledgment of the services of men who had worked
with him as members of his staff, here and there a chair or a department to bear the name of a man so honored. Such gifts did
not involve new adminstrative organizations, merely the boosting
of institutions already in being. Some of his attempts were feeble
and pointless fumblings, the Hero fund for example. What is a
Hero? What is the test of a Hero's heroism? The giving of
money for the building of libraries was more substantial and
2,811 cities were blessed with a Carnegie library all of them much
alike without regard to climate or degree of sunlight. Even so,
a fine new building does not automatically become a blessing
to the community. Only the right books on the shelves and a staff
of trained, sympathetic librarians can bring that about. Nor is it
necessary that they should all be architectural monuments; a

small building in a small town with an intelligent, devoted librarian can do much to raise the human average. Evidently this son of Scotland didn't think much of the church music he had heard; 7,689 churches in the United States and Great Britain received new organs.

At the core of his giving was a firm belief in education. Proof of that was the Foundation for the Advancement of Teaching dedicated to the provision of retirement allowances for college teachers in the United States and Canada. Little thought seems to have been given to advance study of the problem and its dimensions. Small account was taken of the steady increase in college enrollment and consequent additions to faculties and an upward trend in salaries. Additional institutions were put on the list of those receiving grants with little further study. By 1915 it had become evident that radical changes must be made. The fund still operates, but in the form of annuities, to which college, individual professors, the Foundation, now the Teachers' Insurance and Annuity Association, make contributions.

One of the highly useful Carnegie foundations is the Carnegie Institution in Washington for the promotion of research in the physical and biological sciences. The Carnegie Corporation of New York, established in 1911, has for its purpose the "advancement of knowledge and understanding among the peoples of the United States and the British Commonwealth," by grants to colleges and professional and educational organizations usually for specific purposes. This is the largest of the Carnegie funds totalling $125,000,000.

There were two projects in which the old man confessed a special interest that now have a pathetic air, the Endowment for International Peace and the Peace Palace at The Hague. Peace does not come for the wishing or the buildng of a beautiful palace. Henry Ford was later to learn that a Peace Ship would not avail to "call the boys out of the trenches before Christmas." One Carnegie gift must have given him a thrill of poetic revenge. In his poverty-stricken youth in Scotland he had seen and writhed at the snobbish indifference of the lairds of Pittencrieff to the wretchedness of their tenants. His agent at Dunfermline made all the arrangements for the creation of a public park of seventy acres out of the domain of the snobbish lairds and when the deed was done cabled to his principal in New York: "Hail, Laird of Pitten-crieff!"

The Carnegie gifts during his lifetime and by his will amounted to $350,000,000; he had not quite achieved the respectable poverty envisioned by his slogan "The man who dies rich dies disgraced," but he had made a good try at it. How much wisdom does perspective give for an appraisal of this colossal benefaction? To be sure he was a pioneer and necessarily handicapped by the general ignorance of the time as to ways and means of raising the human average, an ignorance which all of us shared. He created many separate funds without adequate provisions for their administration. He was forced to proceed by rule of thumb and the wonder was that the method worked so well. He emphasized too much the permanence of the capital so lavishly set apart. A later giver of a large amount, Julius Rosenwald, flatly declared his inability to peer far into the future to determine the needs of generations yet to be and set ten years as the lifetime of the principal of his fund. The future must take care of its own.

Vague and groping as was his large beneficence, Carnegie set a pattern for the philanthropy of the future. Before the new century had half run its course individuals, families, companies, a widely varied lot with a multitude of objects and stipulations had set up foundations. Tax laws had much to do with this development of course, but it is unquestionable that much weight must be given to a growing sense of the stewardship of wealth that Carnegie had proclaimed. How many of these foundations can be counted today? Perhaps four hundred, perhaps more.

The objects specified cover a wide range, most often of a scientific or welfare character. Out of Utah Copper came three Guggenheim foundations one of which made possible Stephen Vincent Benet's "John Brown's Body," an eloquent narrative poem of the Civil War. A grant from the Rockefeller Foundation built the huge telescope on Mount Palomar in southern California. The

Woodrow Wilson National Fellowship Foundation offers a thousand fellowships annually to first-year graduate students preparing to become college teachers. So the lists of benefaction grow; and the effects on our tax and investment policies are beyond calculating.

One of the more surprising of these funds is the Russell Sage Foundation with assets of thirty million and annual expenditures of approximately a million. Around the turn of the century Russell Sage, "Uncle Russ" to the Wall Street reporters, was a symbol of penny-pinching penuriousness and many tales were told of his peculiarities; the New York *Evening Post* said of him that he was the "village skinflint writ large." The morning paper that he read on the way to his office was one that some other reader had thrown away in the suburban train that bore him to his daily toil. He was a thrifty speculator, and in times when the stock market was more than usually active he dealt largely in call loans to enable brokers to carry their margin trading overnight; sometimes the interest rate on these short time transactions ran as high as twenty-five per cent for twenty-four hours. Uncle Russ deplored such immoral gambling in his public comments and reaped a rich harvest in private.

A story was told of a time when his shrewdness brought him no profit. A blizzard was blowing and he was due at a directors' meeting for a corporation that followed the practice of distributing the total number of gold pieces equally among the directors present and in a howling storm there would be few if any in attendance so Uncle Russ turned up his coat collar and braved the blast. Alas for the vanity of human hopes! For the first time on record there was a full attendance. Evidently there were other penny pinchers.

His fortune was appraised at sixty million dollars and his will named Mrs. Sage as the sole legatee. The Russell Sage Fund is the result of the benevolence of Mrs. Sage, as is the Russell Sage College for Women in Troy, N.Y.

Probably the most sensational of the many large gifts of

that time was of South African origin, the Rhodes Scholarships. Cecil John Rhodes was the fourth son of an Anglican clergyman in Bishop's Strotford in Hertfordshire, England. His father destined him for the church and planned for the necessary university training, but weak lungs made life in the English climate impossible for him. Two of his older brothers were already in South Africa and writing enthusiastically of the hot dry climate and rich soil of Natal. An English doctor gave the seventeen-year old Cecil six months of life in England and he followed his brothers to South Africa. There was a year of cotton growing in that new land and then he joined the rush into the newly found diamond diggings in what was soon to be Kimberley.

America had known many gold rushes since the days of Forty-nine, but nothing quite like this South African adventure. Three civilizations collided there. In 1836 the Boers of Cape Colony, resenting the freeing of their black servants by the British Emancipation Act, had made their big trek into the remote north where they had only natives to contend with. The Boers were a people straight out of the Old Testament, pastoral, dogmatic, unbending in their Calvinistic faith. The only forms of property they recognized were land and cattle, and for these they would fight all comers, but they had failed to reckon with the diamonds of Kimberley. Word of a region where diamonds could be picked from the ground as one digs potatoes spread fast and the inevitable rush began. Many of the diggers were riffraff, men of weak will and little purpose spawned in the slums of London, but along with these came other men, men with hard eyes and grim determination, and Cecil John Rhodes was one of them

Rhodes brought with him the dream of an Oxford degree and in his spare time away from the diggings he studied the map of Africa and slogged away at the Latin and Greek that Oxford demanded. In due course he was accepted at Oriel College. In the cloisters of Oxford he must have seemed as rare a bird as to the other diggers in Kimberley. Oxford terms are shorter than in American colleges and when his fellow students spent the long vacations walking or bicycling about England or the continent with books for summer study, young Rhodes hurried back to Kimberley to gather more diamonds for the nurture of his dream. Even so, he found time for reading, Plato, Marcus Aurelius, Aristotle, some Darwin and always history. It took time, but he gained his degree at long last and was also a wealthy man of prominence in South African affairs.

There was one respect in which Rhodes differed from the men with whom he worked and was beginning to use. The shadow of his early ailment walked with him all the way; there was so much to do and so little time for the doing. As he was dying he whispered to his lifelong friend Leander Starr Jameson, "Dr. Jim: So little done, so much to do." He was not yet fifty when he died; a columnist on a New York newspaper once referred to him as "the *aged* Cecil Rhodes!"

How large was the Rhodes fortune? It was impossible to say. It was a confused and fluid thing, shares in mines and railroads, wide stretches of land, houses and farms, debentures, government bonds. His will provided for trustees with wide discretion. There had been no time for marriage, so there were no direct heirs. His Oxford diploma was much more than a sheet of parchment, it was to be the corner stone of a union of the English-speaking peoples of the world, based on a shared experience of Oxford scholarship. The lion's share of this magnificent benevolence was allocated to the United States, a hundred scholars to sixty for the British colonies and fifteen for Germany. (Rhodes had talked to the Kaiser and hoped to offset the growing antagonism between the two empires; somewhere he had picked up an Americanism — "make a deal.") The original allowance to each man was set at two hundred and fifty pounds per year for a period of three years with no racial or religious discrimination. Wars and currency changes, especially the devaluation of the pound, were to make changes in detail, but the basic plan remains. The annual stipend is now seven hundred and fifty pounds sterling per year to each scholar, $2,150 at the present rate of exchange of $2.80 to the pound. Thirty-two new scholars are appointed each year from the United States. Early fears of failure to measure up to the exacting standards of Oxford have proved groundless and the plan is an assured success. Here, if you please, is an Anglo-American alliance in being.

Rhodes was buried in a rocky amphitheater high up in the Matoppo Hills where he had once sat in council with the Matabele chiefs. Friends had urged him to take a strong force with him in case the chiefs turned ugly. The advice was rejected out of hand. "That would mean war," he said; "I want peace." So he went to the council armed only with a riding crop with a native boy as interpreter at his back. Behind the chiefs stood masses of armed men, the hardest fighters in all Africa. Rhodes talked for hours and came away with the peace he sought.

What is the record of Rhodes scholars in America as viewed in the light of more than fifty years of operation? Liberal education has benefited greatly by this infusion of the spirit and the method of Oxford colleges as is abundantly clear to one who has seen and appraised the contributions made by former Rhodes scholars to the American curricula and techniques. Honors courses have multiplied, a process of which Swarthmore under the leadership of Frank Aydelotte, an early Rhodes scholar, is a shining example. Useful emphasis has been laid on independent work with stress on the ability of the student to use the written word with facility and grace. If Rhodes aimed at an Anglo-American union, as he certainly did, the alliance in two great wars is a gratifying result. Seldom has great wealth been used to better purpose.

> I dream my dream
> By rock and heath and pine
> An Empire to the northward
> Ay, one land
> From Lion's Head to Line

If as sharp a contrast as possible with the Rhodes dream is sought the case of Hetty Green is a strong contender. Hetty died leaving a fortune variously estimated between a hundred million and two hundred million dollars. If her wealth is to be determined by her contribution to a better world she wasn't worth a cent. She may have loved her son Ned and her daughter Sylvia in a twisted selfish way, but all she did for them was to blight their lives as surely as she deformed her own. After years of dodging and suing and lying, the Green estate came into the hands of the Massachusetts Institute of Technology and became a research laboratory for the study of electronics. To the summer people in nearby Salter's Point the red lights blinking on tall masts to warn off low flying planes earned for the old Green homestead the name "Red Light District." To the unscientific observer that is a sufficient memorial.

CHAPTER VI

In the Time of the First Roosevelt

THERE was one figure in that whirling turn of the century that caught the attention of all of us and moved us to praise or blame — Theodore Roosevelt. For more than a decade his words, his ideas, most of all his acts commanded front page position in the most hostile newspapers, and friends and foes alike were violent. His family background offered little reason for anticipating the tumult of controversy that he seemed to engender. His father was a businessman, public spirited, quiet, successful, who had provided the son with an income large enough to insure him against serious fear for the future. Physically the boy was "a sickly and timid child," his own words. As a student at Harvard, where he graduated in 1880, he attracted little attention except for his determined persistence in a course of physical training, boxing, wrestling, fencing, whatever would help develop strength of body and speed of reaction.

After Harvard he read a little law, contemplated a business career, and in 1882 announced his intention of running for the legislature from his district in New York, a mixture of silk stockings on Fifth Avenue and cotton, if any, on lower Sixth. A friendly district leader who knew his way around took him on a tour of the saloons on Sixth, but after a few talks with important saloon keepers in which the youthful candidate announced that he favored a higher charge for saloon licenses, his guide took him away and advised him strongly to forget the saloon vote. To the surprise of his supporters, and still more of his opponents, he was elected, the youngest member of the legislature that year. The press gallery veterans at Albany hailed him with joy. Here was a target made to order for their jibes. He was a fop, a dude, a Lord Dundreary. His clothes, his mannerisms, most of all his Harvard accent were ridiculed and a short career was seen for him. We have been slow to learn that a Harvard accent is not necessarily a political liability.

Those were rough and tumble days at Albany. The Tammany members were riding high, and the upstate Republicans, the "Black Horse Cavalry," were forced to content themselves with such bits and pieces as they could pick up through "deals" with the majority. The young Roosevelt wasn't having any deals which added to the amusement of the old hands in the legislature. At one time he confided to a friend that he thought he would retire from politics at the end of his term. He was not to retire as long as he lived.

After three years in the legislature he was appointed to the Federal Civil Service Commission which was struggling to bring some semblance of order and efficiency to Federal appointments where reform was greatly needed. By this time the young man was beginning to attract attention by the bluntness of his speech and the energy of his acts. What he said he would do he did, and he worked fast. He served on the Commission six years, 1889 to 1895, and earned the praise of two presidents, Cleveland and Harrison. When he left there were 86,000 positions on the "classified" list, meaning that the incumbents were no longer subject to whimsical or partisan removal. Then he moved back to New York to become a member of a bi-partisan police board, one of four. In spite of the inevitable tendency of such a four-horse team to travel in every direction but forward, he brought his driving energy to bear on the almost impossible task of cleaning up the force. Repeatedly he declared that to the man on the beat there was no such thing as a good law or a bad law. Only one question demanded an answer, was it a law? If the answer was "Yes" then it became the business of the policeman to enforce it.

The policeman was not a legislator or judge, he was a law enforcement officer.

As police commissioner Roosevelt became aware of a Danish-born police reporter, Jacob Riis. While the other reporters assigned to cover police news sat in on the unending poker game in the press room across the street from headquarters, Riis poked into dark corners nearby: Five Points, Mulberry Bend, malodorous clusters of cold water flats, breeders of vice and crime, nurseries of disease, and blurted it all out in a book "How the Other Half Lives." Young Roosevelt read the book and never forgot it. To him Riis became "Useful Man Number One." The highly respectable owners of tenement house property in that area had reason to remember the book too. Trinity Church was one of the worst of the offenders.

In the legislature Roosevelt had shown little interest in social problems. A proposal to reduce the hours of workers on traction lines below the standard twelve had left him cold and housing was no concern of the lawmakers. He had been born into the stuffy acquisitive society that had grown up in the North after the Civil War and he had found it quite comfortable. Riis added a chapter to the Roosevelt education, and he began to understand some of the ways in which destruction of the poor is their poverty.

The next move was back to Washington as Assistant Secretary of the Navy. He was a rapid-fire reader of books all his life with a rare gift for gathering useful facts as he leafed his way through a volume and somewhere he had encountered Captain Mahan's "Influence of Sea Power Upon History." This he added to his library and took with him to Washington. At that time Mahan's was a voice crying in the wilderness. The ending of the Civil War had left the American people weary of battle, and Congress cut the Army and Navy appropriations to the bone. For nearly twenty years many graduates from Annapolis had found themselves without ship assignments because there were not enough to go round. Instead of sea duty they were handed a year's pay and the thanks of the government. Most of them disappeared into civil life, but a few drifted out to China and found berths in the new Chinese navy that Li Hung Chang was building to offset the growing strength of Japan.

We believed that our destiny lay on land where railroads were being built and homesteads were multiplying. Our small squadrons were enough to give such representation as we needed in foreign waters, Hong Kong, Yokohama, and the West Indies. Big battleships were for the European powers if they chose that road of national suicide. Roosevelt's superior, John D. Long, was content to take things as he found them. If Congress was satisfied with a small Navy it was all right with him. To his assistant secretary a weak sea force was a disgrace and a danger, and he said so with copious citations from Mahan. A phrase that was often on his lips in later years was "Walk softly and carry a big stick!" That big stick was the Navy. Roosevelt found supporters outside the Department, and a Navy League was formed composed largely of civilians. Wheels began to turn even in Congress and shipyards began to hear of orders.

So matters stood when the battleship *Maine* was sunk in Havana harbor and the look of things changed overnight. When war was declared, the Assistant Secretary of the Navy had already notified Commodore Dewey, the commander of our small squadron in Asiatic waters, to be ready to sail for Manila on an instant's notice. Dewey's brief and victorious action in Manila Bay is now a part of our history, but by that time Roosevelt was no longer assistant secretary of anything. He had cleared his desk and given notice of his intention to raise a regiment of volunteers to be known as the First United States Volunteer Cavalry, but remembered as the Rough Riders. That was surely something new and strange in our military history. The Rough Riders were found on the cattle range, among college athletes, deputy marshals, frontier sheriffs, perhaps a few gunmen and they gave a touch of color and romance to an otherwise dull and fever-stricken spectacle.

For the newspapers that war was a free-for-all with no holds barred. It was known that Spain had a fleet in reserve in home

waters and it was believed to be more powerful than anything
we could muster in Caribbean waters. It was also taken for
granted that it was at large in the Atlantic and about to attack
any or all of our seaboard cities. Boston, New York, Philadelphia
and Baltimore took turns shuddering in terror. We had no planes
or radio for scouting, but we were long on imagination. Young
William Randolph Hearst had lately arrived in New York and
taken over a decrepit old newspaper the *Journal*. He began to
match wits and headlines with Pulitzer's *World*. A faint smear
of smoke that someone thought he saw on the horizon was good
for at least half a column. That was journalistic enterprise in
the "good old days." Hearst sent Frederic Remington, famous
for his drawings of horses and horsemen of the cattle range and
the cavalry, to Key West to provide illustrations for the mounting
drama. The artist soon grew weary of the limited scenery of
Key West and wired his employer for relief on the reasonable
ground that there was no war in sight. Back came a peremptory
order from Hearst: "Stay where you are; you make the pictures
and I'll furnish the war!"

Not all the reporters shared the prevailing hysteria. The
New York *Herald* sent a level-headed veteran who found life on
the shore of a tropic sea quite easy to take. After a few days of
idleness, the cub who had been sent down as leg man for the
old timer wearied of this tropic shore stuff and urged his chief
that a wire be sent now and then. The chief patted the cub on
the arm and assured him that the business of the moment was to
sit in the shade and sip cooling drinks. "We will sip a few more,
then we will stroll along to the telegraph office and there we
will wire Christmas greetings." Presently the fog lifted and it was
learned that Cervera's fleet had crossed the stormy deep and was
lying cozily at anchor in the narrow winding harbor of Santiago.

The next act in this curious war was almost a farce. Outside the harbor mouth were the American ships ready for the
showdown. A young naval lieutenant, Richmond Pearson Hobson, came up with an idea. The Spaniards were in the bottle;

why not put in a cork and keep them there? No sooner said than done. The lieutenant took the battered old freighter *Merrimac* and sank her at what he thought was the right spot, himself being picked out of the water by a Cuban fisherman and given living quarters in El Morro (a combination of fortress and prison on the head-land guarding the harbor mouth) satisfied that the job was well done. But it wasn't. Soon the Spanish fleet made a run for it, keeping clear of the *Merrimac*, and was speedily hammered into scrap by the waiting Yankees. That ended the war.

There was a postcsript to this part of the melodrama. We'd been short of heroes for a long time, and Hobson must have his day. It was a short one. Misguided friends in his home state of Alabama whispered to him of public service in Congress and he became a candidate for the nomination. He came out strong for Prohibition, always a popular political gadget in the South. He was handsome, he spoke well, and his campaign was off to a good start and rolling rapidly until an attractive young lady, a "cousin" of course, threw impulsive arms around the candidate's neck and gave him an enthusiastic kiss. The fever spread, Alabama was full of cousins, and it soon became painfully evident that the Hobson candidacy was fast becoming a joke; the only authentic instance of a promising political career being kissed into oblivion, but not until he had served a term in Congress.

It was the first war our generation had known, and we played our parts awkwardly. Soldiers are traditionally expected to sing patriotic or sentimental songs around the camp fire or on the march. It was proof of our amateurism that we chose for our theme song of battle a popular jingle of the day, "There'll Be a Hot Time in the old Town Tonight." An American living temporarily in Rome was excited by the Italian headlines announcing Dewey's victory at Manila and sought the aid of an Italian friend who spoke excellent, but academic, English and this was the way the Italo-American version came out: "After the firing ceased the American band played 'The Flag with Specks On' and 'It will Be Exceedingly Warm in the City This Evening.' "

While the war went smoothly for us at sea our soldiers found the going on land much rougher. There was turmoil of ships and men at Key West, our port of embarkation, and in the pulling and hauling the Rough Riders managed to slip on board a transport officially assigned to another regiment, leaving their horses behind. When the fleet of transports arrived at Guantanamo Bay there was more confusion and again the Rough Riders sorted themselves out and moved to the attack. As a military force they were informal and short on discipline, but apparently they were experts in the art of taking care of themselves.

The story of the taking of San Juan Hill has been told by men who were there and has no place in this chronicle, but it should be noted that as a result of confusion and misunderstanding of the battle plan men died unnecessarily, but not in the Rough Riders. Their only mistake was in charging up the wrong hill, Kettle instead of San Juan. Meanwhile the Spanish troops in trenches on top of San Juan were dealing roughly with a mixed force of regulars and national guardsmen huddled at the foot of the hill. When a colonel of the regulars sorted that out and led them on to the attack, the Spaniards climbed out of their trenches and legged it for shelter in the city of Santiago.

Another proof of our complete amateurism as makers of war was our service of supply. Uniforms were too heavy for use in the tropics, food soon spoiled in the tropic heat, and medical and surgical supplies were shamefully inadequate. More men died from dysentery and fever than from Spanish bullets. When it was over, Colonel Roosevelt wrote his own account of the affair in a book which Finley Peter Dunne's "Mr. Dooley" called "Alone in Cubia."

As wars go, the Spanish-American imbroglio wasn't much, bush league in fact, but the results were portentous. By the terms of the treaty, Cuba secured her freedom with the assurance of complete independence after a probationary period under our watchful eye, which brought few cheers from American capital viewing greedily the agricultural and mineral resources of the

island. A small group of eager American investors claimed that
the Isle of Pines lying just to the south of Cuba was a separate
entity and large tales were told of its fertile soil, its balmy climate, and its friendly people. It was said that here was the last
stand of the old Roman civil law in the American world, and that
if Cicero happened to come back to earth he could argue cases
in the courts of the island — in eloquent Latin, of course. What
this was supposed to prove was past finding out and this tropic
jewel remained a part of Cuba. Far to the eastward, Puerto
Rico was also ours with a promise of problems for the future.
Half around the world was another possession the Philippines,
an archipelago on the rim of the China Sea. Spain had held these
islands almost since the days of Magellan in spite of chronic rebellion and bushwhacking. To complete the list was the island of
Guam suggesting something by Gilbert and Sullivan. Still another overseas possession came to us in that year of war, but by
purchase and not as a prize of war, Hawaii.

What we couldn't possibly guess was that we had unac-
countably wakened from our long absorption in our own re-
stricted destiny. If we didn't watch our step we might suddenly
become a world power. Rudyard Kipling gave us solemn admonition to "Take up the White Man's burden, ye dare not stoop
to less nor call too loud on freedom to cloak your weariness!"

These things and more were in the making just around the
corner, but the next item on the political agenda was Theodore
Roosevelt. From Rough Rider to governor of the Empire State
was an obvious progression whatever Senator Platt and the Black
Horse Cavalry might think. So governor of New York he became.
For most of his political life, Platt had been the dispenser of pa-
tronage in New York and he took it for granted that this agree-
able relation would continue. In fact, he had already sounded out
one or two possible appointees. As soon as the new governor was
inaugurated the good news was broken to him. At once there were
warnings and rumblings. The new man would do his own select-
ing, of course with polite consideration of the senator's suggestions.

There was one state post for which the senator believed his man was a "must," that of state superintendent of insurance. Of all the state plums this was the ripest and the juiciest and Lou Payn was the boy for it. Still the governor disagreed. Platt was an "easy" boss, which meant only that he was too wise to make a fight in the open so he sat tight Then the governor came up with strong pressure for a public utility franchise tax. To the senator's mind this was outrageous, out of the question. If a street car company must pay a tax for the use of a public street anthing might happen. Even then the senator bided his time. The gubernatorial term in New York is only two years, not a long time for biding. Perhaps a way could be found to get this young upstart out of the senatorial hair.

Platt had not far to seek. The time for presidential nominations was at hand. The Republicans were sure to try for a second term for McKinley, but the vice presidency was wide open and Hanna, chief sponsor for his friend McKinley, might listen to reason. So wires were pulled and wheels began to turn. Another stumbling block was Roosevelt himself. He had just got into his stride as governor and he had no illusions about the vice presidency. It was only a polite term for a lot in a political cemetery and he wanted none of it. Mark Hanna also was unwilling to be a party to such a maneuver. To his way of thinking T.R., was just a cowboy who had blundered into office, unstable, rash, hard to control or guide.

Then a third force began to make itself felt. The Western delegates to the convention were enthusiastic for Roosevelt and their support was valuable. To them the vice presidency was above a governorship. There were plenty of governors, one in every state, but only one vice president and they were backing Roosevelt. T. R. unwillingly withdrew his objections, Hanna recognized the importance of the Western votes, and the senior senator from New York breathed freely. In a moment of unusual jocularity he said that he intended to witness the inaugural ceremonies to "see Teddy take the veil." Hanna may have had his uneasy moments when he considered that a vice president stands only a single heart beat away from the presidency, but that was a chance that must be taken.

Then fate took a hand in this tangled game. McKinley attending the Buffalo Fair was shot by a crazy man, one Leon Czolgolz, and after a few days of apparent improvement suddenly passed from the scene. Hanna had his final say on the way back from the cemetery after the burial of his friend. Glaring at his fellow pallbearers he remarked: "What did I tell you at the convention! Now that damned cowboy is president."

CHAPTER VII

The Rough Rider in the Saddle

THE NEW president gave the customary assurances of continuance of his predecessors' policies, expressed his entire satisfaction with the cabinet as it stood, and several long breaths were drawn by the doubters. The period of calm was not long. Roosevelt's reputation for acting on impulse without time for consideration did him less than justice. His appearance of impulsiveness was more manner than reality, as his many letters, more than a hundred and fifty thousand, abundantly testify, but it was hardly possible that a man of his energy and multitude of interest should be content to follow the placid, humdrum course that had been McKinley's. With T. R., to decide was to act without hesitation or delay. Later he stated his philosophy of presidential power: that the chief executive has and should have the power to do whatever he believed to be in the public interest. Even pugnacious old Andrew Jackson could scarcely have said more.

In his first message to Congress in December 1901, the new president served notice on Congress and the country of the coming of a change from the quiet days of McKinley. Early in the message he spoke of "very serious social problems. The old laws and the old customs, which had almost the binding force of law, were once quite sufficient to regulate the accumulation and distribution of wealth. Since the industrial changes which have so enormously increased the productive power of mankind, they are no longer sufficient."

67

Then he proceeded to particularize some of these problems and their sources; overcapitalization, the lack of publicity, the wide variation of state laws for the formation of corporations, the dangerous growth of monopolistic tendencies. If present powers granted to the executive are insufficient, "then a constitutional amendment should be submitted to confer the power."

The honeymoon was over. The corporate heads and their favorite newspapers cried out in anger that was at least half incredulity. Did that crazy cowboy in the White House really mean all that stuff about controls and publicity and exact capitalization? How could business be done in blindfolds and shackles? If all states were to be required to overhaul their laws for the formation of corporations, how could such states as New Jersey and Delaware make a living?

Of course there were saving clauses here and there in the message, cautioning words against headlong legislation or persecution. The wise Mr. Dooley from his eyrie behind the bar of his Archy Road saloon summed the message up for the ever present Hennessey: "The trusts, says he, are heejous monsthers built up by the inlightened enterprise iv the men who have done so much to advance progress in our beloved country, he says. On one hand I would stamp thim under fut; on the ither hand not so fast." But joking aside it was evident that a lot of fat had been chucked in the fire. The Rough Rider was riding again.

The man in the White House was a skillful politician and a master of publicity. As an illustration, he knew that Monday was a slack day for important news so he habitually timed his more important announcements for release on that day thus insuring a good spot on the front page. Living in that time was a bewildering and stimulating experience, something between a football game and a cyclone. To retrace his course day by day for the nearly eight years of his rule is to keep score on an earthquake. Early in his term there was a strike in the anthracite coal mines of northeastern Pennsylvania which was made to order for testing the new president's philosophy that he should have the power to do whatever he believed to be in the public interest. It was surely in the public interest to make an equitable settlement in the anthracite mines, but what could the president do about it? Strikes were regarded as matters of local concern to be dealt with by the police or at most by the national guard. To be sure Grover Cleveland had sent a regular army force to Chicago in the A.R.U. strike of 1894, but that was on the ground that the strike was interfering with the passage of the mail. That excuse was obviously not valid here, but anthracite coal was important. But while the miners were well led and controlled by their president, John Mitchell, the situation was ticklish. On the side of the operators of the mines there was a grim determination to fight the union to the finish. These labor agitators must be taught their place and the owners were in a strong position being both coal owners and coal carriers. When the anthracite deposits were being developed around Scranton, the railroads of that area had thriftily acquired the mines thus insuring a double-headed control of anthracite wealth.

The operator's philosophy was stated by George F. Baer, the president of the Philadelphia & Reading Railway, in a letter to a W. P. Clark of Wilkes Barre, Pa., July 17, 1902. "The rights and interests of the working man will be cared for and protected — not by the labor agitators but by the Christian men to whom God in His infinite wisdom has given the control of the property interests of the country and upon the successful management of which so much depends." There was the older attitude in a pious nutshell, smug, firm, and arrogant. If God was on the operators' side who could be against them? But for all its orthodox platitudes it was an indiscreet letter as even the conservative newspapers were quick to make clear. The presidential response was equally prompt with the appointment of a joint commission with power to arbitrate between the strikers and the owners. Mitchell, the wise head of the union, immediately accepted the proposal. The owners haggled briefly over the naming of a labor representative as a member of the commission, but this objection was speedily removed by describing the union man an an "eminent sociologist," which must have amused John Mitchell. That turned the trick and the question of constitutionality and divine intent hadn't even been raised.

The case of the Northern Securities Company was a horse of another color. As far back as 1890 a law known as the Sherman Anti-Trust Act had been passed by Congress prohibiting contracts in restraint of trade in interstate commerce. No attempt had been made to enforce it. Richard Olney, the Attorney General, had declared publicly that it was so obviously unconstitutional that he would make no attempt to test it. So the matter rested and dust accumulated on the Sherman Act until 1901 when powerful interests on the floor of the Stock Exchange met in a struggle for the control of the stock of the Northern Pacific Railway. A new figure had appeared on the Street in the person of Edward H. Harriman who challenged the power of J. P. Morgan and James J. Hill, head of the Great Northern Railway. To call it a "titanic battle" would be a considerable understatement. Northern Pacific stock skyrocketed from a modest one hundred dollars a share to a thousand and more N. P. stock changed hands on the floor of the exchange than there was in existence. Then the battlers agreed to cry quits and unite in the formation of a holding company to be called the Northern Securities Company.

Here was a real chance to test the constitutionality of the Sherman Act, and three years later a case came before the Supreme Court on appeal from the U. S. Circuit Court in Minnesota. The decision of the Supreme Court called for the dissolution of the Northern Securities Company as a combination in restraint of trade. There were dissenting opinions by four justices, including Justice Holmes lately come on the bench under appointment by Roosevelt. Holmes based his dissent on the ground that no restraint had been proved, and the majority opinion was purely a speculation in futures. But the court had spoken and the Sherman Anti-Trust Act was in business.

This case marked a milestone in several ways: it was the first

invocation of a law long on the books; it seemed to give the coup
de grace to a new form of corporate organization — the holding
company — but that was only seeming, the holding company is
still with us; it was the first dissent by Justice Holmes who was
to appear in that role on many occasions; most of all it marked
up another victory for T. R., who was likewise to appear often
in that role. Incidentally it would soon become clear that two
strong men at opposite ends of Pennsylvania Avenue did not see
eye to eye in all cases. One thing was sure, this man in the White
House meant what he said about the use of presidential power.
It was about that time that a new governor of Pennsylvania on
being asked to state the policy of his administration made his
cryptic reply: "My policy will be one of celerity tempered by
cunctation." Whatever cunctation the president exercised, his
celerity was obvious as was his growing popularity.

It would serve no useful purpose to recite the long list of
presidential acts that called for front page position or indicate
the items in order of date, but a few are necessary. As a ranch-
man he had viewed the waste and misuse of our natural resources, forests, minerals, water supply and in his seventh message to Congress in December, 1907, he declared: "The conserva-
tion of our natural resources and their proper use constitute the
fundamental problem which underlies almost every other problem
of our national life." Within six months he followed up with
a conference of governors, congressmen, members of the cabinet,
judges, public spirited men to meet in Washington. He opened
the meeting, laid the problem before them, and urged action.
Not much cunctation here but plenty of celerity. In effect he
gave the meeting its program. That was the launching of the
Bureau of Reclamation that has added so immeasurably to the
wealth of our natural resources in irrigated land, water power,
protection of our forests, and national parks and monuments.
Thanks to T. R. wide stretches of desert are now green and
fertile.

There was a heritage of the Spanish-American fracas that we

had viewed and toyed with for a long time to no purpose. This too was now crowded into a place on the Roosevelt program, the need for a canal to cut the narrow neck of land from Atlantic to Pacific. When the war burst upon us our newest and strongest battleship, the *Oregon*, was lying at anchor in San Francisco Bay. Now she must go at top cruising speed all the long way round to the Caribbean where the need was urgent. Seventy-one days she drove south to Cape Horn, north to Cuban waters. She made it in time to edge in on the fight with Cervera's fleet, but the moral was obvious, a transisthmian canal must be built.

But where? And by whom? De Lesseps fresh from his success at Suez took a look at Panama. This was no Suez easily cut through desert sand. A railroad had been built from Colon to Panama but at the cost of a life for every tie in the line. The cost of fever is high and the project languished. There was strong support for a route through Nicaragua at sea level. There would be less digging but more dredging and the cost of maintenance was uncertain. Congressional feet dragged. Was it possible to build locks of the necessary capacity on Panama? The minority thought it was and so the argument droned on. A legacy of our experience in Cuba had been the discovery of the cause of the yellow fever and malaria that had slain their thousands in the De Lesseps experiment. Congress finally saw the light and conceded the possibility of the Panama route.

Now another difficulty presented itself, Colombia. Panama was a province of Colombia and we were reasonably popular at Bogota, capital of Colombia, but Colombia's relation with her province was an uneasy one, as a reputed record of fifty-three revolutions in fifty-three years bore witness. There was no overland route from the mother state to the turbulent daughter and Colombia was willing to sell her equity, such as it was, of course at a good price. So the bargaining began. Unfortunately for Colombia there was a man in the White House who had no love for the chaffering of the market and when the inevitable revolution broke out in Panama, November 3, 1903, events moved fast and on November 18, 1903, the new republic of Panama signed a treatly granting a canal zone to the United States which was ratified three months later.

Colombia yelled to high heaven for justice and the critics of T.R. pointed to the close sequence of revolution, recognition, treaty, canal. Did the man in the White House have guilty knowledge of the revolution before it happened? Did he perhaps help to set the stage for the drama? It was difficult to dig up much sympathy for the bargainers in Bogota. It was clear that what that capital saw in the situation was the chance for a top price for a piece of real estate that had hitherto been more liability than asset. The Colombians had had their chance and muffed it. T. R. said only, "Yes, I took the Isthmus."

Even at this late date it is not possible to separate the tangled factors in the Panama episode. Stock in the old De Lesseps Panama Company had been widely bought by people who were reaping a large profit from the Suez holdings. But no one seemed to know who these stockholders were. A certain Philippe Bunau-Varilla purported to represent them but both he and his American counsel, William Nelson Cromwell, stalled and bargained over names and amounts. What was the value of the old De Lesseps equity in Panama? Was it ten million or forty? It was rumored incidentally that Mr. Cromwell's fee was eight hundred thousand. Bunau-Varilla was plausible but vague. Colombia managed transport by sea for a military force as far as Colon at the Atlantic end of the Panama railroad, but American marines were strangely unable to arrange transportation to Panama where the revolution was centered. Long after the canal was in full operation the United States paid Colombia the tidy sum of twenty-five million dollars for whatever rights Colombia asserted.

In retrospect it seems impossible that the canal should not have been built by American capital and operated under American control. Each year eleven thousand ships pass through the canal east and west and at the southern tip of the continent old Cape Horn looks out over an empty ocean. But the canal would have been hard digging had it not been for the services of Col. William C. Gorgas in his war on the germ-carrying mosquito. Even so there were many false starts until army engineers under Gen. Goethals took over and did the job.

Probably T. R.'s busiest year was 1905. The canal was still in the making when the water around the island of Santo Domingo began to boil with trouble. European creditors were threatening action to collect overdue debts. The Monroe Doctrine said nothing about Uncle Sam's duty as a collection agency, but T. R. sent a force of marines to see what they could do. So far it was only a teapot tempest but it might easily become much more than that — which it ultimately did.

Added to these items the Russo-Japanese war began to worry the expert worriers. Russia was losing all along the line, Newchwang, Port Arthur, Mukden. Then came Admiral Rojestvensky whose fleet had been gathering barnacles in the Baltic, now under orders to seek glory somewhere around Japan. On the way out there was an "incident" calculated to amuse only the higher of the high gods. Scarcely clear of the waters of the Baltic the Russians sighted the Japanese fleet. It was really a fleet of English trawlers a long way short of Japan, but the Russians manned their guns and let fly. That was one naval fight the Russians won. In Tsushima Straits they met the real Japanese and that was the end of Rojestvensky's search for glory — also the end of the Russian navy.

It was obvious to anyone of intelligence that the Russians were losing the war, in fact had already lost it; only the Russians disagreed. Perhaps if they lost Mukden they might get the idea but that would put the Japanese in full control of Manchuria and on the march to Vladivostok. That would really spill the beans for certain European powers, including Japan's ally Great Britain. The stage was set for friendly intervention in the interests of peace. We were loud in our praise of the Japanese; our term for them was "those wonderful little people," but wasn't there a possibility that they were beginning to believe it themselves?

The traditional procedure at a time like this was for one of the major powers of Europe to tender her good services in the cause of peace. Unfortunately there was a man in the White House who was making traditions of his own and T. R. jumped the gun. To be sure there was a canal in the making and a revolution threatening in Santo Domingo, but this was only one thing more and it might be exciting. The European powers were not sorry to see the sprawling Russian giant take a dusting but they were relieved to see someone else jump in. There was a whirlwind of letter writing, many to the Kaiser, a few to the Czar, to the Japanese, many to the shifty De Witte, chief spokesman for the Russians, an imposing but hollow figure, a few to Edward VII of Great Britain, and of course many to T. R.'s close friend Henry Cabot Lodge and to another confidant, the English historian George Otto Trevelyan, nephew of Macauley.

The President found De Witte less than dependable. What he said today had little relation to what he would say tomorrow, and it was often in direct contradiction. Under no circumstances would he admit that his country could lose the war. On the other hand the Japanese were definite, trustworthy, logical. T. R. found a sympathetic correspondent in the German Kaiser. Whatever the French and English statesmen thought of him the American president got on with him famously; they seemed to speak the same language.

So the wheels of correspondence revolved. There were so many things to cover. Where should the representatives of the belligerent powers meet (Portsmouth, N.H., was chosen). Who should outline the agenda of the meetings? What should the terms of settlement be? Who should fix them? T. R. was in his element, having a "bully" time. The usual phrase was for the intervening power to "proffer our good offices," but that had to be stretched to cover T. R.'s expansive dimensions. He not only proffered his good offices, he almost rammed them down the throats of the warring powers. He suggested possible terms of settlement and hinted to the Japanese that they keep their de-

mands for territory as modest as possible, perhaps only half the
island of Sakhalin.

We on the sidelines looked on with interest and admiration but little thought that this peace conference might ultimately concern us greatly, although there were signs if we had had the wisdom to read them. About that time I had a pleasant interview with Baron Kentaro Kaneko, a financial representative of Japan operating in the United States. One question I asked had to do with the future status of Manchuria. This, the Baron assured me, would be open to the trade of the world, which was much more than the Russians had ever conceded. Another question was about Korea, now entirely in Japanese hands. There was a perceptible drop in the temperature of the interview as the Baron assured me that here was something entirely different. "The Koreans are a broken, degraded, helpless people," he said, "whom we must protect and develop. They will be a heavy burden to my country for a long time, but that is one of the liabilities of this war." I quoted this in my report of the interview but without special emphasis. For a world power we were curiously naive. The conference dragged the usual weary length and ended with a treaty that presently was abrogated by the logic of later circumstances. We the unseeing observers of history in the making turned our attention to other and lesser things.

CHAPTER VIII

The End of an Era

THE FINAL phase of the career of Theodore Roosevelt was marked by a surprising naivete compounded by assumptions that were ridiculous for a man with a reputation for hard-headed realism. As the campaign of 1908 approached the president announced that he intended to observe the two-term tradition although only one of his terms had been elective. There was nothing wrong with this. There is no law requiring a man to run for office against his will. But coupled with this was an implication that as soon as his "second" term was completed he was dropping back to the status of an ordinary citizen and that was not so easy to swallow. We have had many ex-presidents who have taken their own courses after retiring. Jefferson, for whom T. R. had no admiration, had gone to his Monticello lookout, having seen to it that his Secretary of State, James Madison was in the White House. After Madison came James Monroe, Madison's Secretary of State, and after Monroe, John Quincy Adams, Monroe's Secretary of State, the best in our history and the terminal point of the Jeffersonian dynasty. When Adams retired it was into the House of Representatives as member from Braintree, Massachusetts, and a sturdy fighter for the right of petition against the Southern members, a real elder statesman and our only one.

Generally speaking we have not been greatly concerned about our ex-presidents, conceding them the empty role of Elder Statesmen but paying little attention to them otherwise. Why couldn't this incumbent go the same quiet way? Apparently it was not in his nature to do aything quietly, retiring least of all. His decision to retire to private life was followed closely by an announcement of his intention to join the long list of African big game hunters. That too was front page news, as were the personnel of his safari, his camp library — bound in pigskin — his equipment, also the fact that no reporters would accompany him; he would be his own reporter. All this was something new in presidential routine, as was the intimation that he was giving serious thought to the identity of his successor. There have been other cases before and since when the retiring executive has given a strong hint of the man who would make a worthy successor, but this was more of a hint than usual, almost a dictate.

The course followed is much clearer in retrospect than was the case at the time. William Howard Taft, one time popular governor general of the Philippines, was the man finally chosen but only after much searching. T. R. had favored Elihu Root as his first choice but Root knew only too well that his high standing as counsel for large corporations practically unsuited him as a presidential candidate and he said so promptly. Governor Hughes of New York was given careful consideration as a possibility but he showed no sign of willingness to be an echo of T.R., and the moving finger finally rested on Taft. Taft was politically inexperienced never having been a candidate for popular favor. He was ideally fitted for an administrative or judicial post, an inclination that Roosevelt was aware of. Here he would be on familiar ground and could hardly fail to be a success; he later proved it. His father had been a good judge in Ohio and the son vastly preferred to follow in the father's footsteps, but there were two people who viewed the judgeship with distaste, Taft's brother Charles and his own wife. The latter made no secret of her desire to see her husband in the White House — and herself in the post of First Lady. When that came about no time was lost in staffing the White House with colored servants in livery designed by the First Lady.

The choice of Taft as successor having been made T. R. set himself to groom his man for the task which the candidate viewed with something less than enthusiasm. Only a supreme egoist could have believed in the possibility of such a course of training. Here were two men cast in basically different moulds; Roosevelt, the coach, confident, driving, moving easily from idea to act, Taft the pupil, large, naturally deliberate, slow, tolerant, humorus, ideally made for the bench, as his mother well knew and his wife refused to believe. The coach rehearsed for the benefit of the pupil his own well learned technique of the platform, a somewhat boisterous opening line for the whistle stop, the importance of remembering the names of men he had never heard of and was sure to forget, especially local celebrities. As T. R. saw it the plan was obvious. A local committee of welcome would board the train at a previous stop and T. R. would ask for names, preferably a guide, fisherman, bear hunter, and when the president appeared on the platform he would call out the name of the local worthy, preferably a nickname, and "Old Bill" would be pushed forward grinning from ear to ear. Such an approach was a natural for T. R. and it never failed; Taft for all the coaching usually forgot the name or hopelessly bungled it. Along with this elementary course in the steps necessary to win votes on the road went consideration of the importance of good appointments from which followed perceptible hints that the new president would be wise to continue the existing cabinet.

To have believed that he, the coach, could so completely remake the basic characteristics of a mature man with positive ideas of his own was incredibly naive, an assumption of the ability — and the right — to make a president who should be the reflection of his own image. It was a thing that couldn't be done and shouldn't have been tried, but T. R. believed that he had done it and went on with the preparations for his African adventure convinced that he was passing his power on to safe hands. The handmade candidate became president and the ex-president set sail for Africa and private life. (On the day he sailed there was a last flare of the old antagonism when a sign was displayed on the floor of the New York Stock Exchange, "Wall Street expects every lion to do his duty!")

The inevitable difficulty was not long in appearing. One of the former president's appointments was of Gifford Pinchot as the head of the newly created Bureau of Forestry in the Department of the Interior. Pinchot was a man of the Roosevelt stripe, stubborn, energetic, firm in his belief in the righteousness of his own views and when he encountered opposition from the head of the Department, R. A. Ballinger, he appealed to the president for support against the secretary. It was at bottom a petty squabble over the disposition of certain coal lands in Alaska and after some investigation the president upheld the secretary and Pinchot was asked to resign. When news of this rift within the lute was passed on to the big game hunter the reaction can be only remotely imagined; clearly something was awry with this chief executive that he had created after his own likeness.

With his African hunt behind him Roosevelt returned to his version of private life by delivering a lecture at Khartoum on the upper Nile where doomed "Chinese" Gordon made his last stand against the forces of the Mahdi. In general he praised the British for the manner in which they had borne the white man's burden with a few references to things that he would have done differently. There was another lecture with more advice at Cairo, a short stay in Rome, and a "bully" experience with the Kaiser in the course of a grand review of the German army. Thence to England, an address at Oxford and a degree of D.C.L. His privacy was beginning to resemble a post as an adviser at large to the powers of Europe.

It is not necessary to trace the steps by which T. R. moved on to an open break with the successor whom he himself had so carefully prepared. Attempts by influential friends of both men to heal the breach were futile and events moved rapidly on to the campaign of 1912 and a showdown in the Republican convention of that year. An inexplicable speech by the president at a meeting of midwestern farmers at Winona, Minn., had aroused violent criticism among opponents of the Payne-Aldrich bill, a high protective tariff measure. Taft had assured newspaper correspondents that he proposed to take a strong stand against this bill and copies of his speech had been distributed in advance, thus lightening the burden of the reporters covering the meeting. To the consternation of all his hearers the speech that was given was a complete contradiction of the one expected. The Payne-Aldrich bill was praised and his listeners were assured that all was well in Washington. What had happened to change the presidential mind was never made clear but there were the inevitable rumors of undue influence. Taft seemed blandly unaware that anything out of the ordinary had occurred. Senator Dolliver of Iowa, wise in the ways of Washington, said of him: "He is an amiable gentleman entirely surrounded by men who know exactly what they want."

Mr. Dooley behind the bar in his Archy Road saloon put the Payne-Aldrich bill in focus with his blistering summary: "The Republican party has been true to its promises. Look at the free list if ye don't believe it. Practically iverything nicessary to existence comes in free. Here it is. Curling stones, teeth, sea moss, newspapers, nux vomica, Pulu, canary bird seed, divydivy, spunk, hog bristles, marshmallows, silkworm eggs, stilts, skeletons, and leeches. The new tariff bill puts these familyar commodyties within the reach of all."

In the regular Republic convention of 1912 the backers of Roosevelt did their best to swing the votes of the delegates to T.R., whether his second or third term was of no importance. Taft was nominated and the supporters of Roosevelt walked out and set about the forming of a third party which should be known as the Progressive, more often called the Bull Moose Party from a characteristic remark by T. R. when he was asked how he felt, "I feel like a bull moose!" Such priority as Senator LaFollette of Wisconsin might have claimed to the label "Progressive" was lost in the shuffle.

A convention of the new party was called for a fortnight later. In his opening speech T. R. used a phrase that was often quoted: "We stand at Armageddon and we battle for the Lord!" Here was the naivete of all time, a party squabble compared with the final battle of the forces of Good against Evil which should determine the future of the races of mankind.   Whether the Progressives battled for the Lord or not they made substantial contribution to the sweeping Democratic victory that followed. Roosevelt received eighty-eight electoral votes to Taft's eight. Woodrow Wilson came in with four hundred and thirty-five. An attempt was made in 1916 to nominate T. R. again but he didn't even appear at the convention.

There was one more high spot in this man's career less naive and more commendable. When the United States entered the war in 1917 the old warhorse sniffed the wind blowing from the battlefields of France and announced his inention to form a legion of sportsmen to ride over the trenches as the Rough Riders had climbed San Juan hill and applied to the president for approval. Gen. Pershing to whom the proposal was passed along promptly vetoed the idea. The old naivete was present in the assumption that such a force, many of them in their fifties or even sixties, could endure the strain and boredom and filth of the trenches. That ordeal was for young men only, but the impulse that prompted the offer was worthy of all praise.

What was he like down inside, this man Roosevelt? To a large extent we are all enigmas to each other, Theodore Roosevelt probably more than most. To his friends and admirers, of whom there were many, he was a knight in shining armor without fear or reproach, the herald of a new day. To his critics, of whom also there were many, he was a destroyer, a public enemy. One sample occurs to this chronicler. A prominent railroad official remarked that he had been invited to the White House along with other railroad men to talk with the president but he wasn't going. To the question why not the answer came hot and hard: "Everyone says that if you meet him you can't help liking him, and damn him, I want to hate him." The time is long past for raking over the ashes of such old fires, but it is still in order to look back along the years for his essential characteristics.

Henry Adams said of him that he was all Act. That much is sure. It is hard to find any clear examples of concern with the philosophical aspects of his acts. He found life exciting — or he made it so — but he gave little indication of powers of analysis of himself or of others and his judgment of others was sometimes deplorable. He seemed to have drunk deep of the fountain of youth and he was always in motion. Henry Pringle who wrote an excellent biography of him said he was "violently adolescent." John Morley the English philosopher-historian saw him as a combination of St. Paul and St. Vitus. Later on Morley amended this by saying: "He is more than American; he is America." There was large room for doubt there. T. R. was far from being the typical American. For this honor, if it is an honor, there were better candidates, LaFollette, McKinley, Mark Hanna, even Bryan. Once a friend calling at the White House and finding Mrs. Roosevelt preparing to leave with the children for Sagamore Hill inquired casually if Theodore was going with her to meet a prompt retort: "No, and for heaven's sake don't put the idea in his head. That would make just one more child to look after." Elihu Root who knew T. R. and liked him made ironic comment on his discovery of the Ten Commandments. T. R. said of himself once that he was just an ordinary man raised to the ninth power.

Perhaps as a result of his childhood weakness and timidity he set himself to be an exponent of the Strenuous Life. "Hit the line hard." "Clean as a hound's tooth." "I feel like a bull moose." "Walk softly and carry a big stick." These were favorite phrases. He was capable of autohypnosis to an extraordinary degree. He and his friends were always on the side of righteousness and the other fellows were supporters of evil. After the dust had settled on Panama he declared that his negotiations there were "in accordance with the highest principles of national, international, and private morality." Even a cursory glance over the tangle of intrigue, evasion, charge, and counter charge, the dubious correlation of revolution, recognition, and treaty reveals the basic absurdity of such a sweeping statement.

The squabble with President Taft over the displacement of Gifford Pinchot had a postscript in the time of the later Roosevelt. Harold Ickes, Secretary of the Interior for Franklin Roosevelt and a former supporter of Theodore, took the trouble to go carefully over the official record of the Pinchot episode and to his surprise found himself agreeing with the presidential action that T. R. had found beyond pardon. Pinchot was his friend and could do no wrong. "Malefactors of great wealth" was a favorite term with him. In spite of his early doubts of the "cowboy president" Mark Hanna supported him loyally nevertheless his name was in the malefactor category.

Early in his administration he had announced his philosophy of presidential power which was in general to do whatever was necessary in the public interest. There was nothing extraordinary in this. Most strong presidents, notably Jackson, Lincoln, Cleveland, might have said the same thing but hardly as gleefully as did this one. Afterwards he told with delight of an occasion when he signed a presidential order withdrawing 16,-000,000 acres of public land from private entry, then immediately after signed a bill prohibiting a president from doing what he had just done. His comment was typical: "Opponents of the Forest Service turned handsprings in their wrath."

The right to determine the public interest belonged primarily to the president and the judiciary must walk with care. When Justice Holmes whom he had appointed with some misgivings wrote a strong dissenting opinion in the Northern Securities case he made no secret of his regret over the selection of Holmes and when a higher court reversed Judge Landis' decision tagging Standard Oil with a tidy $29,240,000 fine he complained that the bench was assuming too much power.

Inherent in his concept of the Strenuous Life was a deep admiration of the virtues developed in war. No Prussian warlord could more loudly sound the praise of the warrior than did this American president. His selection of Scriptural phrases was significant, "The sword of the Lord and of Gideon." "We stand at Armageddon and we battle for the Lord." In his category of days the best of all was the day he spent on San Juan Hill facing the Spanish fire. This was no martial pose or pretense.

Next to war his favorite phrases were taken from the vigorous field of sports, "Hit the line hard," "Clean as a hound's tooth," "My hat is in the ring," "Stripped to the buff." A favorite artist was Gutson Borglum monumental sculptor and patron of the prize ring. When John Singer Sargent painted his portrait he posed him standing on the lower step of a staircase gripping the newel post as though about to wrench it from its place. His personal courage and will to endure were beyond doubt, as he showed in his African hunts and later in the exhausting struggles in the South American jungle along the "River of Doubt." When his youngest son Quentin was shot down in air combat over France he paid eloquent tribute, "He died like an eagle fighting in high air!" Here again was the essential Roosevelt voicing his resentment of the dullness of material success that won the hearts of the young men of his era. He was only sixty-two when he died but he had packed a lot of living into those swift years.

CHAPTER IX

Jerome the Crusader

WILLIAM Travers Jerome gave hope and courage to the young men of Manhattan as Theodore Roosevelt challenged the young men of the country as a whole. We knew that we were citizens of a great city and a sinful one. Tammany was in the saddle and riding hard. Gambling and prostitution were commonplaces in many cities, but in New York it was the police who decided where and at what price vice should flourish. The police captain who did not at least double his pay with his share of the protection money taken from gambling dens and brothels was too dumb to be a captain long. Richard Croker was at the head of Tammany and smiled at the efforts of hopeful reformers to oust him. Here and there a clergyman ventured a rather feeble denunciation of police corruption, but far too many of them looked the other way. Many good citizens refused to take reform seriously. There were guesses at the total amount paid for police protection, but they were only guesses. Madams paid high rent for rattletrap tenements and the respectable owners of such property collected the rent regularly, smiled, and said nothing. If you didn't like vice why not stay away from it? Commercial travelers of that time preferred an "open" town; it was "good for business."

There was one clergyman who refused to hold his tongue. That was Charles F. Parkhurst in his church on Madison Square. Gradually he collected evidence of widespread police corruption and spread it before his congregation on Sunday. The man who won't be stopped, can't be stopped and finally the legislature at Albany appointed a committee to investigate the Parkhurst charges. This committee under the chairmanship of Senator Lexow began to turn up something that looked like business. One police captain who was then in the Tenderloin precinct repented himself of his part in this ghastly comedy. That was Schmittberger, fundamentally an honest man, who was glad to be clear of this tangle of protection and collection and he stayed honest.

The work of the Lexow committee was thorough and the echoes of it lasted a long time, and the man who was chiefly responsible for that was the chief counsel John W. Goff. Goff was a dramatic figure. Irish born and self-educated, he hated England with a deadly hatred. As a young man he became an active Fenian and helped to organize an armed force to strike at Britain through Canada. Of course the adventure got nowhere; Britain remained undisturbed and the invaders faded away. Lawyer Goff became "Recorder" Goff, the last man to hold that title in the New York courts. There are probably a few old men still living to whom it is unnecessary to do more than mention the title "Recorder" to be at once understood.

I was once drawn on a special panel for jurors in Goff's court. I was engaged at that time in a vain attempt to shore up a crumbling publishing business that was determined to die. It was not that I dreaded jury service. In fact I wished for nothing better than to see the Recorder in action but I didn't dare desert my post of duty and I gained a hearing through the recorder's secretary. I had my moment in a corridor lined with bailiffs and suppliants. I found myself facing a tall gaunt figure in a red gown that made him look every inch the "hanging judge" that many lawyers called him. I hurriedly stated my case and he spoke a few words of mild reproof about the duty of a good citizen and he granted my plea. It was soon over but I have never forgotten the fire in the old eyes.

As a cross examiner Goff had no equals and he drove relentlessly through the chevaux de frise of lies and weak evasions that the recreant policemen offered. One police captain explained an inflated income by ascribing it to real estate investments in Japan. Boss Croker decided that his failing health made this a good time to take a long vacation in his castle in Ireland. The police protection of prostitution was badly crippled though not fatally, but it would never be so open and unashamed as before the time of Lexow.

One of the young lawyers on the staff of Goff was William Travers Jerome who was to become a marked man. He was a distant cousin of the mother of Winston Churchill, also marked for greatness. In the regime of King Tammany the district attorney's office had been a catchall for indolent lawyers who clung to the coattails of a district leader. The formula was simple: "This is my friend Jimmy Phelan. He's a good boy. Do what you can for him." From a district leader in the days of Tammany's power this mild request was a command. In consequence the district attorney's office slumbered while complaints and charges piled up and there were only unimportant indictments reported from grand juries. Clearly there was need for drastic housecleaning.

In the year 1901 young Jerome threw his hat into the ring for the office of district attorney of New York. Seth Low, a wealthy merchant and one time president of Columbia University, was nominated for mayor. That was an opening for ambitious and enterprising young men and I stepped forward as an apprentice campaigner. To my surprise I found it absorbing and stimulating. I was always a little on the glib side and my chief handicap was complete ignorance of politics in New York or anywhere else. But I was a quick learner and I had a lot of fun. Meetings were sometimes held in small halls but generally on the street from the flat bed of a truck. A night is recalled when our platform was in a covered truck. I wondered why the cover but I soon learned. Our location that night was in the West Fifties generally called Hell's Kitchen, a region where there was to be found an explosive mixture of races, chiefly Negro and Irish with a pinch of other alien strains; the cans and bottles that rained down on the top of our truck were known to the police as "Irish confetti."

Incidentally I closed my part of the campaign by getting arrested on a blanket charge of illegal registration. An old roster of students in Columbia University was the evidence. At the Fifty-Fourth Street court I was shoved in the pen that contained the harvest of the night, drunk and disorderly, petty thievery, wife beating, a cutting or two, the sweepings of the street. My detention was brief. A word from a plain clothes man standing by, a curt "Dismissed!" from the judge and my term in jail ended.

That campaign was a strenuous one. Seth Low, the reform candidate for mayor was eminently respectable, sententious, and dull, but Jerome provided enough fireworks for everybody. As a member of John Goff's staff he knew the story of police graft from beginning to end. Here was something new in the political world, young, lean as an athlete, magnetic, he drew men to him automatically and his crowds grew. He was almost a chain smoker, cigarettes usually, and he made no secret of an occasional highball. His opponents aimed their fire at his personal habits. He was seen at a bar throwing dice for the drinks and that made him a gambler. He ignored these thrusts, save for the occasional gibe that he thought he was doing fairly well on a diet of cigarettes and Scotch highballs.

The election of 1901 was a complete victory for reform from top to bottom. Jerome wiped the slate clean in the district attorney's office. The old hangers-on who enjoyed the support of district leaders went down the drain and new men appeared, young, able, ambitious, and honest. Complaints that had been gathering dust in the files for months were hauled out and sent along to the grand jury and there began to be convictions. The district attorney's staff worked long hours. Jerome demanded three things of his young men, intelligence, honesty, and unremitting work. As fast as they showed themselves competent they were given a free hand with prompt support when they called for it. One of his best men was Arthur Train who said of his chief that his was a synthetic personality, a mixture of Savonarola, St. George, and Dartagnan. His belief in himself was so great that sometimes he seemed on the point of regarding himself as the only honest man in sight.

Generally he was for the under dog, the little man who had no powerful friends and his assistants went along with him. I once sat in a jury box while Train tried a case that hinged on the question of the defendants' status; was he a dealer in business for himself or was he an agent? He was young with the look of a beaten man weary and without hope. The complainant by contrast was a bloodhound hot on the trail. Train's attitude was that the lone man had already suffered enough and we of the jury brought in a verdict of not guilty of the offense charged in the indictment which was grand larceny. At least one of the twelve men good and true has never felt the faintest twinge of regret for his part in that act of mercy.

New York newspaper editors generally supported Jerome, but there were two exceptions, Hearst of the *Journal* and Pulitzer of the *World*. Hearst's opposition could be credited to political ambitions of his own. Pulitzer's case was a trifle mysterious but something of his attitude could be charged to his insistence that action be taken against the large insurance companies and the traction combines. In due course these would be attended to but not by Jerome.

New York had many German citizens who held to their Old Country habit of frequenting beer gardens especially on Sunday afternoons or evenings. It was a harmless pastime and a friendly one, but the rigid Sabbatarians frowned upon it and thought that the district attorney or the police or someone should do something about it. The district attorney refused to be interested and the police had enough on their hands without bothering about a few German beer drinkers. So the Germans continued to sip their beer in peace.

Gambling was another matter and Jerome hit the gambling

places hard. Most of them were little fellows and the evidence against them was easy to get, but there was one big fish who eluded the district attorney's net for a long time. That was Richard Canfield, prince of all gamblers. He had palatial rooms next door to Delmonico's, the deluxe restaurant of the day. Finally an under cover member of the district attorney's staff wormed his way into Canfield's rooms and a raid was planned. Came the night. Canfield's doors and windows were known to be barred, but acetylene torches took good care of that. Jerome dined at Delmonico's to be near at hand. A window was forced, a ladder was pushed through, and Jerome in dinner clothes stepped inside to find Canfield and his lawyer, also in dinner clothes, sitting comfortably in a beautifully furnished room with no sign of gambling apparatus anywhere around. "Good evening, Mr. Jerome," said the gambler. "Good evening, Mr. Canfield," said the district attorney. Members of the invading group made a careful search of the rooms without result until a locked door of a closet called attention to itself. The door was broken down and there was revealed the needed evidence, cards, roulette wheels, all the tools of the gamblers' trade. That ended Canfield in New York county although he operated in Saratoga for some time, enabling customers to lose their money on the ponies in the afternoon and on roulette in the evening.

The cause celebre that Jerome himself tried and which filled much of his time for more than two years was the killing of Stanford White by Harry Thaw. White was a distinguished architect and Thaw the somewhat degenerate offshoot of Pittsburgh millions. Jerome set himself to convict Thaw of first degree murder and turned himself into a student of alienism to meet the expected plea of insanity. Meanwhile the many friends of White, gourmet and popular host, ran and hid. There was one notable exception and that was Richard Harding Davis, writer, correspondent, and himself a romantic figure, young, handsome, fit, an athlete who was always in training. Never an intimate friend of Stanford White, his sense of fair play was

outraged by the chorus of denunciation of the architect and he
stood up and spoke his mind. He was not to escape unscathed.
A librarian in a small New Jersey town decided to do his bit
in defense of American womanhood and ordered that all books by
Richard Harding Davis be dumped in the gutter where, he
asserted, they belonged.

The trial of Thaw was a field day for sensational reporters
who rang the changes on the theme of the gallantry of the aber-
rant boy in coming so bravely to the defense of American womanhood as represented by Evelyn Nesbit whom White had so ruth-
lessly wronged. Peter Dunne's "Mr. Dooley" paid his ironic respect to "these desprit journalists that had pledged their fortunes
and their sacred honor, and many of thim their watches, to be
prisint and protect the public agin the degradin' facts."

There were two women intimately concerned in the outcome of the trial whom the sensation-mongers left severely alone.
One of them was Mrs. Thaw, the mother of Harry, whose only
offense was her loyalty to her son and her firm belief that he was
the object of the district attorney's persecution. The other was
Evelyn Nesbit's mother who, as was shown, had brought her
attractive daughter to New York as to a market place. Much of
the time it was hard to tell whether the case was being tried in the
courtroom or in the newspapers. Jerome refused to be diverted
or annoyed by the atmosphere that enveloped the whole troupe of
incidental performers. Early in the trial it became clear that the
defense intended to concentrate on a plea of insanity and Jerome's
work on alienism began to pay dividends. Many of the "experts"
called by the defense were at least half frauds. Strange terms
appeared; "emotional insanity" was one, "adolescent insanity"
was another. "Brain storm" belongs to this case, another was the
"higher law." Under the pressure of Jerome's informed examin-
ation the users of these weird terms became confused and incohe-
rent. One of Jerome's witnesses, a real alienist, remarked later
that Jerome was the best alienist he had ever known among
lawyers. In spite of the efforts of the defense to show that their

client was insane for the moment only, Thaw was convicted and sentenced to confinement in the Matteawan Hospital for the criminal insane.

Before we the innocent bystanders had more than time enough to draw a long breath, Thaw escaped from the presumably well guarded asylum and was smuggled across the line into Canada. The hunt was up again. The Canadian officials were correct and cooperative and raised no obstacle to extradition but in Canada, as in New York, the run of the mine citizens rallied to the defense of the persecuted hero. Once Jerome was seen throwing dice for the drinks and was arrested as a public gambler. The magistrate before whom he was taken discharged him at once with profound apology. Thaw went back to his Matteawan cell.

It is scarcely worthwhile to trace the course of this long and baffling case. The public lost interest, Miss Nesbit alternately feared Thaw and scorned him. The dew was off her pitiful romance and she wanted to be left alone. Even Thaw's mother confessed that she could no longer continue the fight and that she wanted nothing so much as to have her son kept in permanent restraint. Now the sensation seekers were looking elsewhere for material for their pipe dreams. Somewhere there was an end of this case that had held the stage for far too long a time.

There were other cases, mostly routine charges and pleas, but there was one wild one, involving Morse, a dubious gambler-promoter whose lawyer was Abe Hummel, a shrewd New York defense attorney for whose scalp Jerome had been reaching ever since he had become district attorney. At one point in the proceedings it became important to the defense to smuggle a witness across the border into Mexico and to Jerome to take him to New York. Every expedient was brought into play and before the comedy ended United States marshals, Texas Rangers, and once a gang of local toughs calling themselves the Wharton County Woodpeckers took part. In the end Jerome won the case and Mr. Morse was put on ice.

Jerome seemed made to order for a larger political field than district attorney and he was clearly in agreement. Some of his friends believed him a natural for governor. He had just what Albany needed, but he was too unpredictable, too hard to hold, and the state bosses turned thumbs down on him; he retired to private practice after eight years as district attorney. As counsel and director of an early motion picture enterprise he helped nurse it through the uncertainties of corporate childhood and lived to see it reach a lusty and profitable maturity. But no one who had known him as district attorney could ever forget him.

CHAPTER X

Whirlwinds of Change

IN 1894 Henry Adams, the gloomy historian and author of
"The Education of Henry Adams," declared that there had
been more changes since 1854 than in the whole recorded history
of mankind prior to that time. That may well have been true;
what is certain is that in our time around the turn of the century
there was a special sense of something that to us seemed revolutionary. Consider a few of the more important and visible forces:
the automobile, the aeroplane, the radio. There were other things
that changed us but few that approximated the monumental
effect of these three in our world.

Before the appearance of the automobile, good roads were
practically unknown outside the larger towns. We country people plugged along through mud and dust and snow as they
came. If the roads were too bad we stayed at home or plodded
along on foot or horseback. We of the younger set occasionally
achieved a bicycle and there were bicycle races with trick riders
and freak wheels carrying up to a dozen riders; these were to
give a touch of comedy to the occasion. The first wheels to appear
were the old high wheeled variety with a small wheel hitched
on behind to help the rider keep his balance. Even with that improvement merely to mount one was an acrobatic feat and to stay
on board for most of us a matter of luck. A variation of this was
something that seems to have called itself the Star. This had
the small wheel in front, but it found few takers. The real bicycle age began with the appearance of the modern low wheeled

type just before the century made its turn. Roads were still bad in bad weather but bicycle paths appeared here and there alongside a few roads.

A large industry grew up around the bicycle with favorite makes, Columbia, Pope-Hartford, New Era, and the like. Ambitious young men who managed to reel off a hundred miles in a single day gained the right to wear a special badge provided by the League of American Wheelmen. George Fitch, the creator of "Old Siwash" and a college friend of this narrator, boasted four or five such decorations, but most of us were more modest. Accommodating railroads carried bicycles in the baggage cars free of charge and lines running into large cities on pleasant summer Sunday afternoons carried crowds of bicyclists returning from a day of fresh air and wayside picnics.

Of course there were prophets of doom as always crying Woe! Woe! These merry people were desecrating the Sabbath. Why weren't they in church repenting their sins or at home sleeping off the effects of a huge Sunday dinner? Those were mostly Protestants; Catholic padres called attention to their early services and otherwise kept their hands off the wheelmen. The sensible apparel that women wore for cycling was mannish and suggestive and the close association with men was destroying their feminine gentleness and making them as coarse as were the men. Medical journals feared the effect of cycling on the health of women — which incidentally was never better.

It would be an error to think that the automobile swept in like a flood and washed the bicycles and their riders away. In fact, the bicycle is still with us as the racks provided outside public schools give ample testimony, and riding a bicycle on the sidewalk is still a misdemeanor. Trolleys had become a common means of transportation well before the end of the old century, but the first decade of the new brought a variation of the trolley that filled a serious gap in our transportation map. This was the interurban trolley. In the middle west the main railroad lines from all points of the compass focused in the larger cities, chiefly in Chicago, which by 1900 was the hub of a vast wheel of steel. This was all very well for dwellers on the spokes of the wheel, but what about those in the places between the spokes? That was where the interurban came in. Trolley lines appeared running "cross country" from spoke to spoke and farm wives found it an easy way to run into town for bit of shopping in spite of mud or dust; small towns that had merely nodded to each other at a distance found themselves in close daily communication. Not passenger service only was provided but also express and freight, and trolley fortunes grew.

For the longer runs there were buffet dining cars and even sleeping cars. The sleepers were a revelation to travelers who had known only the stuffy Pullmans and the jerking and hammering of steam traffic. The easy swaying of the trolley literally rocked the occupants to sleep. The real garden for the rapid blooming of the interurban was in the middle western states where distances were greater and the wheel design of main railway lines more clearly marked. Time was passing and the automobile was coming nearer, but we had not yet realized its nearness.

There was another change that came so gently and imperceptibly that few of us saw it coming. The expiration of the basic patent that had given the Bell Company its long monopoly opened the way for independent lines and telephone instruments began to appear on farmhouse walls that previously had known no such decoration. With a trolley line at the door and a telephone in the kitchen what more could the farmer want?

The automobile had its genesis among German scientists, but it was the French who first sensed its possibilities and began to explore the possible market. It was still clearly a rich man's toy and its use and enjoyment were limited to the paved streets of the larger cities. In England there had been many experiments with steam traction on the well made roads that the lumbering but romantic old stage coaches demanded and drivers damned the sporting newcomers as a menace to the nervous horses and laws were enacted requiring that a man with a red flag walk ahead of the traction engine. Rolls, one of the English motor pioneers, long remembered those troubled days when his powerful car was compelled to idle along at the speed of a man on foot.

In this country there were few laws limiting speed on the highway, but none were needed. The roads themselves took care of that. There was the factor of price too; not many of us could afford such a costly plaything for our few leisure hours and the early American cars were mostly in the luxury class. In general, designers followed the style of carriage makers in building the body with a curved dash board and even a whip socket at the right of the dashboard. Steam had its supporters among experimenters, and Stanley steamers had many ardent advocates, but in 1900 two names appeared that were soon to become famous, Ransome E. Olds and Henry Ford. Olds announced his intention to speed up production to the dizzy peak of five cars a day; quantity production had arrived among us.

Henry Ford began as the operator of a bicycle repair shop and in leisure hours built a small car by hand. The son of a farmer and himself a poor man he was by inclination and experience interested in the possibility of a low priced car and bent all his efforts in that direction, at one time offering his famous Model T at a price of $310. Long before the new century was ten years old he was a marked man and his eccentricities were front page news. He raised the wages of his workers to five dollars a day eliciting screams of pain and prophesies of bankruptcy from his rivals. He bought a newspaper in his home town, the Dearborn *Independent*, and used it as a personal organ. He hated labor unions and fought them for years, finally under growing pressure coming to terms with them. Somewhere he encountered a weird document known as the Protocols of Zion purporting to lay down the plan of a worldwide conspiracy of wealthy Jews for the enslavement of the world. He stated on the witness stand that "history was bunk." He was vulnerable at many points, but he brought down the price of his automobiles so that the little men on farms and in small towns were moved to dig themselves out of the mud and he made it possible for the workers in his factories to own the cars that they had helped to build. It was the Ford factory that led to the discovery that quantity production demands quantity consumption. From then on the grid of concrete roads spreads over the country. As a minor result his fortune was estimated at a billion dollars.

Of course there were prophets of disaster as there always are when men are venturing from the known into the unknown striving to learn the things "we are not supposed to know." It was said of the early railroads that the speed of twenty-five miles an hour would wreck the nerve system of the passengers. What of these demons of the highway that internal combustion engines had released? Would any of us be safe? Newspapers printed catroons showing the bodies of the dead in the wake of a speeding automobile. It must be admitted that on that score our record is not too good, due in large part to our lax administration of drivers' licenses. To be sure motor roads have invaded wilderness haunts hitherto sacred to campers and wilderness wanderers, but they have given a taste of the wild to the motorists from crowded towns, so perhaps the balance there is even. The horse, once the shaper of our lives, is no more and our lives are the easier for the change. Take it or leave it we are living in a motor age and on the whole liking it.

Close on the heels of the automobile came the aeroplane, also a product of the internal combustion engine as was the automobile. To fly like a bird was a dream older than Christendom. The legend of Icarus is beyond dating. That universal genius Leonardo da Vinci, supreme in many things, painting, sculpture, architecture, engineering, drew plans and specifications for a "flying machine," but as with other dreamers his product lacked the power to lift it into the air and remained earthbound and helpless, waiting for the plodding German scientists to come along with the internal combustion motor. DaVinci was forced to content himself with the building of the first wheelbarrow.

In this country there were experimenters who were coming

closer to a solution of the problem. Simon P. Langley thought something could be done by starting with a glider only to land ingloriously in the muddy Potomac to the accompaniment of jeers and stingy advice. The sage Chicago *Tribune* assured its readers that there was no chance that man would fly "until we become angels." The Boston *Herald* smugly advised the hapless flyer to give his attention to diving and submarines. The ridicule broke poor Langley's heart, but later he received the recognition and praise he deserved — posthumously of course.

It was left to two brothers in Dayton, Ohio, Orville and Wilbur Wright, to be the designers and builders of the first aeroplane. The Wrights like Henry Ford came out of a bicycle repair shop to try their luck in the air. They had studied the writings of Octave Chanute who had worked out his calculations on the drafting board and in the laboratory, and the brothers set about the testing of the Chanute theories. They found a place in the sand dunes of Kitty Hawk, North Carolina, where they had space and privacy. On December 17, 1903, a reporter for a New York newspaper wired his editor that he had seen one of the brothers rise in the air for a sustained flight of more than a hundred feet. His editor promptly wired back advising him to have nothing more to do with the local brew.

Whatever the merits of the local brew in North Carolina, man was in the air after the long dreaming and two obscure Americans had put him there, but we were at a loss to know what to do next and we did nothing much, although a few crazy daredevils like Glenn Curtiss and Augustus Post risked their necks. About that time I talked with Post about flying and learned to my surprise that he had found no thrill in planes. There are three perfect ways of travel, he declared, horse, canoe, and balloon. These alone gave a feeling of intimate relation with the vehicle and of quick response to the occupant's slightest movement. By contrast, driving a plane was little different from driving an engine on a rigid road of iron.

Although Americans had been the first to fly, the rest of us were not much impressed after the first flurry; it was the imaginative French who took up the task. Our army and navy people were supremely indifferent. What was flying to them? If rapid movement of troops was necessary there was always the faithful horse. In fact when the army stirred unwillingly from its lethargy the few planes were lumped with the cavalry. Proper dress called for spurs hence the officers assigned to the new wing continued to wear spurs. Newspaper humorists explained that the purpose of the spurs was to keep the wearer's feet from slipping off the desk top and waking the daring aeronaut from his pleasant dreaming.

The navy was even more indifferent. They had battleships, cruisers, and destroyers and needed nothing more. One dissenter appeared among army officers, Billy Mitchell, who was goaded finally to assert that bombers would be built powerful enough to sink the most powerful battlewagon from the air. He was ridiculed by most of us, court martialed and suspended from the service. (In the second World War, Japanese flyers were to demonstrate the Mitchell thesis at the expense of the *Prince of Wales*, England's greatest battleship. When we entered the first World War we were forced to borrow planes from the French and British. They were crude affairs those early fighters looking like chicken crates with wings, but they gave notice that planes were here to stay.

I saw my first planes at Belmont Park on Long Island in the fall of 1909. The feature event of the afternoon was a race from Belmont Park around the Statue of Liberty and back to the field. That was the year that Louis Bleriot flew across the English Channel.

Except for exhibition purposes ("barnstorming"), such things as privately owned planes were unheard of and regular schedules and routes were out of the question, and it would be a long time before even the largest cities began to take thought of an airport. Flying called for large space for taking off and landing, special training for pilots, and special navigational facilities in the air and on the ground. It was the first World War which ended many things that gave the big initial push to the aeroplane. Now the air force has a department of its own to match the army and navy in the training of officers.

In December, 1901, it was announced that an Italian engineer, Guglielmo Marconi, had sent a message by air from Glace Bay, Nova Scotia, to Clifden, Ireland. It was brief, that first message, merely the letter S, but it was significant, the germ of a mighty growth. Unlike the automobile and the aeroplane, the radio was the work of trained engineers instead of groping amateurs. Marconi's performance was the result of years of study and experiment. In common with his colleagues he knew what he wanted and moved steadily to its achievement.

It would be a waste of time to compare these three engines of change, the automobile, the plane, and the radio. Which has made the largest contribution to this civilization of ours? Take your choice. The first harnessed the internal combustion motor and set it to the service of man. The radio matched the speed of light and Puck's proud boast that he could throw a girdle round the earth in forty minutes was far outmoded. A man in New York or Washington would presently speak with a friend in Moscow or Singapore as though they stood face to face so far had we come from the creeping adventure of Magellan. A motley crew of messages, broadcasts, radar, sonar, television comedies, advertisements of toothpaste, news of life or death was in the making

Not all the forces of change were mechanical. In 1905 a group of men in Chicago met for lunch and agreed to unite for weekly meetings at which men of diverse callings might sit together to join hands across the barriers of work and interest. That was the beginning of Rotary International and the first of the luncheon clubs that have become such a prominent feature of American life. Other groups followed suit and Rotary spread around the world and similar clubs with different names, Kiwanis, Lions, and the like appeared, all with similar ends, the forming of acquaintances outside the area of each man's individual occupation. All profess high standards of community service and call themselves "service clubs." Rotary alone has five hundred thousand members in ten thousand clubs located in 116 different countries.

It is easy to ridicule these clubs. There is much horse play, absurd rules requiring attendance, the use of first names or nicknames, levying fines for trivial offenses, the singing of club doggerel hitched to fine old tunes. There is absurd pride in the observance of trifling rules, but they have added much to the color and friendliness of American life.

There was another feature of American life in 1908 that was an importation from England, the Boy Scouts. General Baden-Powell was a veteran of the war with the Boers in South Africa. That war had been a rude shock to the British. A handful of Dutch farmers had stopped crack British troops instead of cowering in terror as had been expected. Of course the humble Tommy had been blamed for the debacle instead of the real culprits who were the officers. Foot soldiers had been sent in company front, shoulder to shoulder in carefully dressed ranks against a foe they couldn't see. The bearded farmers lay behind stone walls or in dry water courses and shot down the close-locked lines at ranges of a thousand yards or more with aimed fire as they shot game on the high veldt. Wherever the fault lay, something should be done about it and General Baden-Powell set about the organization of something to be called the Boy Scouts to rehabilitate the youth of England. All were agreed that the young had become weedy and indifferent. Rudyard Kipling had damned them as "flanneled fols at the wickets and muddied oafs at the goals," not knowing in how few years these flanneled fools and muddied oafs would give exhibitions of courage and endurance that the English would never forget.

The movement soon spread to this country and there were Cub Scouts and Sea Scouts and presently Girl Scouts, each group under the leadership of men and women of competence and devotion. Each troop was an informal school for the practice of the pioneer arts of firemaking, cooking, camping, and hiking. There were Scout salutes and Scout uniforms adding greatly to the picturesqueness of the countryside; there were Scout oaths whose observance went far beyond the perfunctory salute to the flag. The scout "good deed for the day" was both an obligation and an act of courtesy and kindness.

An institution that should be bracketed with the Scouts was the summer camp. This came later, but stemmed from the same root, the desire to take the young back to a knowledge of the ways and the skills on an earlier day when the wilderness was at our doors. Camps multiplied rapidly and soon the roads of Maine, New Hampshire, and Vermont blossomed with such signs as Keewaytin, Weyanegonic, Aloha. New England is full of lakes and mountains providing the proper geographic setting. A typical camp day begins with the early morning dip, an almost universal requirement. After breakfast small groups under the leadership of experienced counsellors set about their various projects, mountain-climbing, sailing, forestry, rudimentary geology, whatever the environment makes possible. There are separate camps for boys and girls and even for infants, sometimes called the Cradle. For rainy days there are weaving, wood or metal working, play rehearsals, dancing. There are seldom hours enough for all the activities that clamor for attention.

Children in the camps learn to live and work together without rancor and free from the often domineering oversight of parents. The camp season is through July and August and copious tears are shed when the summer ends. Friendships are formed that endure through later life and camp ties are fully as lasting as those among college classmates. Costs vary widely and there are camps for nearly every income bracket. Churches and other religious organizations, the Y.M. and Y.W., provide camps at nominal cost and there are scholarships for foreign campers, usually with no color or race lines. Children from tenement streets acquire at least a nodding acquaintance with a life that would otherwise be hopelessly alien to them.

It was around the turn of the century that golf appeared in America. At first this game, a transplantation from Scotland, was viewed as a rich man's exclusive property. The first club was formed in a New York suburb by a few men who had learned about the game in England and a very exclusive affair it was, but not for long. Young men lower down in the income scale began to press for a chance to learn. New York City led off with a public course at Van Cortland Park, part of a new Metropolitan Park system. The movement spread to other cities until today there is scarcely a community so small and isolated as to be without its golf course.

The overall of these movements into the open air and away from the humdrum life of shops and offices is to call increasing attention to the value of vacations. Part of the old creed of the American businessman was the sanctity of work. He was proud of the fact that he took no vacation and had not for "forty years." The older men viewed the new emphasis on fresh air and moderate exercises with alarm. These young fellows were slackers, idlers, and would come to no good end. Then the older men died of heart failure or liver complaint and younger men with stronger hearts and more active livers took their places. Winter sports drew these "idlers" and skis stepped into line with golf clubs, to the incidental benefit of dwellers in New Hampshire and Vermont who had rooms and food for skiers. Railroads ran special ski trains into the snow-covered hills and young businessmen are proud of their prowess on the long runners. And the average length of life soared upward.

CHAPTER XI

Revivalism in America

A FEATURE of American life that has become an accepted part of it is revivalism. In fact it might almost be said that the prelude to the American Revolution was a revival that got on the records as the Great Awakening. English born George Whitefield appeared in the southern colonies about 1740 and moved northward to attack the rock hard New England Puritanism at its Boston center. Even Jonathan Edwards, the stubborn philosopher of the Puritan faith, was forced to concede a certain plausability to Whitefield. The Whitefield appeal laid strong emphasis on conversion as a means of grace. The fathers of Puritanism had been proud of the fact that the doors of the church were not easily opened, and hardly a third of the adult male population were members in good standing.

The westward movement following close on the heels of the Revolution carried revivalism with it is as a natural part of American life. Along the frontier there were no large halls for meetings, so the camp meeting was born. Peter Cartwright whose autobiography is the classic document of this feature of our history, was converted at a mammoth camp meeting at Cane Ridge, Kentucky, and spent his life preaching and baptizing his many converts. It is part of the record that at one such meeting nine separate pulpits were erected in a large grove and preaching went on twenty-four hours at a stretch. Sinners were stricken as by convulsions. A dominant note in the pioneer preacher's exhortations was his pride in his lack of education or training of any kind; the grace of God was enough.

Gangs of drunken toughs sometimes invaded the groves and free fights ensued. Cartwright was a central figure of that noisy scene on more than one occasion and was not unwilling to take a strong hand in such bouts. Between revivals he traveled widely about the contryside on horseback, sleeping wherever night overtook him with his saddle for a pillow. Most of the state of Illinois from Springfield to the Ohio was his parish. It was his boast that in a single year he had ridden from Cairo to Galena, four hundred miles away, twenty - four times. The small house in which he ultimately made his home is now preserved as a historic monument.

A feature of that time which was still in evidence around the turn of the century was an intense denominationalism. Doctrinal differences were emphasized, especially the importance of the form of baptism; this might easily make the difference between salvation and a futile gesture. The Christian church (we outsiders called them Campbellites) stood fast for immersion and of course proved the case by carefully selected texts. Baptists also were strong for immersion, but held that the New Life began with conversion, while the Campbellites viewed such a concession as a nambypamby shuffle.

The last half of the old century had been a period of far-flung missionary effort also marked by strong denominationalism. It was not enough to bear the Gospel to the heathen sitting in darkness, but it should bear the proper label. We were well along in the new century before a change became apparent. The heads of the Baptist missionary organization discovered to their horror that a large district in India was without a Baptist orphanage and steps must be taken to repair this deplorable condition. Naturally these steps led straight to the office of John D. Rockefeller, Jr., a lifelong Baptist. The outcome was a coldblooded report from the Rockefeller office that though there was no Baptist orphanage the region in question was well served by representatives of other faiths and that Mr. Rockefeller was not interested in entering upon a campaign of denominational rivalry.

Dwight L. Moody struck a nondenominational note just be-

fore the new century dawned; perhaps interdenominational would
be a better term. Moody was a Yankee businessman who was
making a comfortable income when he decided to become an evangelist. He refused to fit into any denominational category. He
took his stand firmly on a union platform requiring the participation of all Protestant sects in the organization and conduct of his
meetings. An important feature of the Moody meetings was the
singing led by Ira D. Sankey and the names of Moody and Sankey were usually bracketed suggesting a vaudeville team to the
minds of the ungodly.

It must be said that sensationalism was a part of the program of the revivalists as it had been in the earlier camp meetings.
This was particularly true of the meetings staged later by the
renowned Billy Sunday. Sunday had been a professional baseball
player and a good one, with no training in theology or public
speaking, and his performance spoke loudly of his athletic prowess. To the trained speaker he was more circus acrobat than
preacher, and the purist was likely to be offended by his physical
antics, but to the surprise of this chronicler in his one visit to a
Billy Sunday meeting, his leaping to a chair or table and back
to the floor was such a graceful exhibition of perfect coordina-
tion and physical fitness that it failed to offend. He used music
to good effect as had Moody, but kept it secondary to his own part.

As had Moody he defied classification by denomination or
creed. The first condition he imposed upon a community seeking
to enlist his services was local participation of all Protestant sects
and the building of a special tabernacle for the meetings. Naturally, these were not architectural marvels, merely bare board
structures with a platform and rows of hard benches with no
decoration to distract the eye of the repentant sinner. Where
the earlier suppliants had been urged to come forward to the
"mourners' bench," in the Sunday meetings the invitation was to
"hit the sawdust trail." Local workers moved about among the
benches making personal appeals to supplement the efforts of the
speaker. It was clear to any observer that Billy was in charge
every minute, policing his own meetings. The slightest sign of

inattention, a coughing fit, a crying baby, was reason for directing the offender to find the way to the nearest exit.

Even in the most fevered moments there were interludes of unintended humor. One meeting found a college boy, a football husky and the son of a minister, the target of a worker's appeal to hit the sawdust trail and become a Christian. Resenting such branding of himself as a heathen, the lad attempted a reply in what was meant as a stage whisper, but came out a bellow: "Hell! I am a Christian." This small incident illustrates the confusion of the time in the use of the term Christian. What was a Christian? What was not? Were we a Christian nation? A baby was brought forward for baptism in a church in a Connecticut town in the time of Thomas Jefferson's presidency. When the minister asked the name of the infant the proud father answered, "Thomas Jefferson." "No such unChristian name in this church", thundered the minister. John Adams, I baptize thee" . . . . And yet Jefferson was our only president to display more than a formal interest in religion.

The substance of Billy's exhortations was of the simplest order, his examples drawn from the everyday world of his hearers, "Quit your meanness, hit the sawdust trail." Simple as it was, it was amazingly effective. Young people gave up dancing and abjured cards at least for the time being. Old offenders shunned the flowing bowl and dropped the use of their favorite oaths. No attempt was made by the evangelist to form a permanent organization of the converts. That was for local churches to take care of. Many of these old sinners stood fast in the newfound faith and became a hard core of fundamentalism in the existing congregations, keeping a vigilant eye on the minister lest he stray from the straight and narrow way of their own thinking. How permanent were these conversions? That's anybody's guess.

A figure of prominence in the college world around the turn of the century was John R. Mott, founder and long time head of the World Student Federation, an outgrowth of the college Y.M.C.A. His slogan was the "World for Christ in this generation." Millions were dying with no knowledge of the true way of salvation. How much if anything did Mott owe to the revivalists? So far as Billy Sunday and his ilk were concerned, nothing at all. Mott was hard, dour, brooding, where they were volatile, pyrotechnic. He was too seriously concerned in his mission to waste time or energy on such childish matters as entertaining or rabble rousing. That was for the lightminded, the spectacular. He was a tremendous worker with a clear sense of organization. As a businessman he would have been a great success, perhaps another Rockefeller. While the grim threat of war darkened the skies all over the world there is no doubt that the effects of his work were deep and wide, however skeptical the observer may be about the possibility of achieving the conversion of this tumultuous world by organization. When he shared a Nobel peace prize with Emily Balch in 1946, he may have had rueful thoughts about the vanity of human hopes.

In any attempt to appraise the typical religious belief of Americans at that time, and probably since, the conclusion is unescapable that it is basically fundamentalist with the revival as the favorite technique. Consider the bewildering array of denominational divisions in the "Yearbook of American Churches" resembling the splinter groups in Communism. Here and there may be found struggling examples of the traditional Anglican persuasion and only in New England is there much evidence of intellectual appeals of the Unitarian variety. The seeker after salvation of the simple brand has his choice in a wide field of predominantly simple requirements, confessions of sins, conversion, and some form of baptism.

Around prohibition there had swirled a long controversy and a Prohibition party had fought valiantly to gain recognition on the official ballot for President, but to no avail. Despite their appeals they remained a splinter group, one of many. Now a powerful church influence and the Antisaloon League took a hand in the conflict with a Bishop Cannon at its head and Rockefeller money behind it. Organization and publicity are strong weapons. League files contained dossiers on opposition members of state legislatures showing with chapter and verse the varied peccadilloes of the men in question. Hints were dropped of possible revelations. This was especially the case in New York, a pivotal state. Usually hints were enough. Correspondents at Albany did not fail to note that the annual legislators' dinner after ratification of the Eighteenth Amendment was the wettest on record. Legislators might vote dry, but they dined the other way. To put it bluntly, they were blackmailed. Those who remember the days of the rum-runners, gangsters, and hijackers may draw their own conclusions as to the services rendered by the Anti-Saloon League.

Another ethno-social phenomenon of that turn of the century was Lucy Page Gaston's anti-cigarette campaign. It may have lacked the expert leadership of the prohibition movement, but it had its features. Miss Gaston rang all the changes on the evils of the cigarette, the deadly effect of a drop of nicotine on the tongue of a dog for example, the habit-forming tendency of the drugs contained in the wrapper of the "coffin nail"; in some places the use or possession of the "makings" was forbidden. Compared with the battle for the ratification of the eighteenth amendment, its effect was not widespread or calamitous, merely a local annoyance. Only two states are recalled as taking action: Indiana and Kansas. It remained largely the personal crusade of Miss Gaston and it soon disappeared. In no sense is it to be regarded as a forerunner of the later controversy among scientists as to the possible relation of the cigarette to cancer, but it was another illustration of our national addiction to the practice of fitting shackles to the freedom that we praise so highly.

Miss Gaston's day in the sun was a short one to be likened perhaps to the career of Carrie Nation, that battling daughter of Kansas who proposed to slay the demon rum with her hatchet. She didn't quite slay the demon, but she broke a lot of saloon windows. The opposition to the cigarette lasted long. When the first world war came upon us, and the War Department decided to turn the operation of canteens over to the Y.M.C.A., the heads of that organization hailed the move as a golden opportunity. "A marvelous chance to reach young men for Christ," said one of them. It was also a chance to minister to tired, wet, cold, hungry

boys back from a tour in the front line trenches.   But should they
stoop to selling cigarettes?   They actually thought they had a
chance to refuse, those Y.M.C.A. leaders, but they were wrong.
The day of Lucy Page Gaston was gone.   If there was danger in
the cigarette it was not for the weary boys just back from the
front.

A distinctive note in the somewhat discordant symphony of
that time was struck by the Salvation Army.   "General" William
Booth had been ordained as a minister of the Methodist New
Connection, an obscure sect in England, but he was too powerful
an individualist to stay long within denominational bounds and
soon separated himself from all organized churches and began
to devote himself to social evangelism, beginning with a small
mission in the crowded East End of London.   That seemed too
narrow a field for Booth's expansive spirit.   By 1878 he had
organized his Salvation Army whose mission was the "salvation
of mankind from all forms of spiritual, moral, and temporal dis-
tress."   While he lived, he was the dominant figure of the movement, the commanding officer and chief of staff.   Local leaders
were officers of different grades and new converts were "cadets."
Distinctive uniforms were prescribed, groups marched in military
formation to the sound of a bugle or the tap of a drum; the hymns
were often written to popular tunes of the day.   Vachel Lindsay,
the wandering minstrel from Springfield, Ill., contributed a poem
"General Booth Enters Heaven," and the opening lines intoned
most effectively by the poet were, "Booth marched boldly with his
big bass drum. 'Are you washed in the blood of the lamb?' "

Requirements for enlistment in this army of the Lord were
simple, a pledge to temperate and unselfish living, glad obedience
to orders, and devotion to the work of the army.   No distinction
was made between the sexes.   Meetings were held in the street
when the weather permitted and groups of the devout speaking,
praying, singing as traffic swirled by were common sights even
in small towns.   There was ridicule to which the workers made
no reply except to redouble their zeal in the work.

In all its activities, the Salvation Army held to its original concept of help to the needy wherever they were to be found. Present membership in the United States is in excess of 250,000 and local organizations are active in most foreign countries. The ridicule of early days has passed and the Army is a fixture in our modern civilization.

A feature of the pivotal year 1900 was the Rev. Charles M. Sheldon's experiment in publishing a newspaper as Christ would have it. For a week the Topeka, Kansas, *Daily Capital* was such a paper. The result was a triumph of promotion and publicity. Churches and religious organizations of all kinds joined in and the average daily circulation of the *Capital* jumped from 11,000 to 160,000. Editorially, this bizarre feat pleased only the temporary editor and the members of his flock. The ubiquitous Mr. Dooley summed up the fantastic combination of piety and publicity with salty wisdom: "News is sin and sin is news," said Dooley.

CHAPTER XII

Books and Writers

THE GREAT Brahmins of New England, Longfellow, Lowell, Holmes, Whittier, Emerson, and their contemporaries cast long shadows, but by the turn of the century other names began to be heard. Newspapers and magazines were multiplying fast and the preeminence of their attitudes and standards was being challenged. Our debt to English writers and styles had been great, but in this new day a much wider range appeared.

Of all the names in the history of American letters none shines more brightly than that of Samuel Langhorne Clemens (Mark Twain). It was not so much that he offered new models to follow as that he drew his material from native sources. Such books as "Life on the Mississippi," "Hucklberry Finn," "Tom Sawyer," and "Roughing It" are not only interesting yarns but vivid chapters in the history of America. His choice of subject matter and his use of the vernacular were something new and endlessly fascinating with its spirited assertion of something that could be called Americanism. To English readers, "A Yankee at King Arthur's Court" could appear as bumptious and irritating. The spectacle of an impudent young American weeping at the grave of Adam in "Innocents Abroad" was absurd, but his refusal to bow to the old and the venerated gave pleasure to his fellow countrymen. It was not so much that young writers began to imitate him — he was inimitable — as that he had called attention to a rich vein of treasure in our own land.

Another man who exerted a large influence at that time was William Dean Howells whose sympathetic counsel and wise suggestions should have earned for him the title of Dean of American Letters. His own writing had wide acceptance and as editor of the *Atlantic*, and later of *Harper's*, he had a keen eye for promising youngsters at a time when the unknown writer had scant welcome in many of the older publishing houses. Sponsoring the new and unknown has its liabilities as Howells learned when he brought a group of the Brahmins together at a dinner to meet the young Clemens. In his speech of response the guest of honor described a gathering of tramps and ne'er-do-wells in a gold camp barroom somewhere in the Rockies. As the comedy developed, it became evident that these frowsy old bums were in reality the Brahmins who were listening to him. The friendly faces around the board froze in outrage and Howells longed to seek shelter under the table. Clemens felt the chill, but was unable to abandon his chosen course.

Embarrassing as it must have been to the people concerned, the episode had a deeper significance. In that quiet room was being dramatized the confronting of the old and dignified and fixed by the new and raw and fluid. What was good clean fun in a Nevada mining town was sheer blasphemy in stately Boston.

Howells was a perfect link between the old and the new. He was a middle westerner, Ohio by birth, and he had been a consul in Italy long enough to share the Brahmin affection for the writers of that mellow land. He was living in Cambridge at the time when Longfellow was working on his translation of Dante, and he was a member of the little group of friendly critics who met weekly at the Longfellow home to discuss the progress of that ambitious project. It was a fortunate chance — or the inscrutable working of destiny — that brought together in Cambridge such an extraordinary group of poets, scholars, philosophers, scientists, teachers as Longfellow, Holmes, Francis J. Child, the elder Henry James, Charles Eliot Norton, Louis Agassiz, Richard Henry Dana. If the Brahminical era was ending, it was signalizing its going with a flowering like that of no other time in our history.

Howells in his editorial chair at the *Atlantic* knew them all, walked with them, talked with them. Nearly every issue of the magazine carried the work of one or more of them. Howells reveled in their company, but always with the sense that a new day was at hand that he would help usher in. The new writers of that day as we drew near the turn of the century were profoundly ignorant of Dante or the Alhambra or the Norse sagas. The beginning of a literature that was to be purely American might well be set at that time.

A surprising feature of that time was the sudden flowering of historical romance. *McClure's* helped to find the way. One of the McClure finds was Booth Tarkington's "Monsieur Beaucaire," more fantasy than romance. His "Gentleman from Indiana" also appeared in *McClure's*, but Beaucaire was his only venture in the purely historical field. He was extraordinarily skillful in finding both comedy and tragedy in the people and things of everyday life. Much of his material came out of his native Indiana as those who remember "Alice Adams" can testify.

He had a keen sense of humor, sometimes taking the form of riotous practical jokes in which he and Harry Leon Wilson, another writer of lively fiction, joined; but usually only a droll comment with a touch of Indiana drawl in his tone. A humorless young Englishman had won temporary fame by walking alone from the Cape to Cairo over the route that Cecil Rhodes had envisioned for his Cape to Cairo railway. When Tarkington was introduced to the young adventurer he looked at him with mild curiosity; "Walked from the Cape to Cairo, did you? All the way? Didn't you get tired?" What could the Englishman say? He had the wisdom to say nothing.

Anthony Hope's "Prisoner of Zenda," also a serial in *McClure's*, was a good sample of the highly imaginary historical romance of the time. In general, the technique was simple: an imaginary kingdom, with a beautiful princess in need of succor. The aid always appeared in the form of a personable young Englishman or American, preferably an accomplished swordsman and linguist.

Another creator of imaginary kingdoms was George Barr McCutcheon with "Beverly of Graustark." He also hailed from Indiana. His brother, John, won undying fame as a cartoonist on the staff of the Chicago Tribune. There was a forerunner to the genre of historical romance, Robert Louis Stevenson's "Prince Otto." For this critic, once an addict of Stevenson, that is still the best of the lot, and perhaps the best of Stevenson. Owing nothing to sword play or archaic speech it is a pure idyll of life in an imaginary world; and it is still worth reading.

Mary Johnston, a young woman in Virginia, wrote "To Have and to Hold" that had wide acceptance. Here was no imaginary kingdom, but colonial Virginia in the time when indentured servants were being brought into the colony by the shipload. Here was romance with a solid footing in history. Ellen Glasgow was another Virginia woman who made solid and lasting contribution to the sum total of American literature. Born in the first decade after the war that destroyed the old South, she grew up in a Virginia that knew the breakdown of the old and the hard struggle back to something new. Her novels dealt mostly with that theme and her last "In This Our Life" was awarded the Pulitzer Prize in 1941.

A weakness of much of the historical fiction of that time was the unwillingness or inability of the writers to do the necessary digging into historical sources, but there were two notable exceptions: R. Tait McKenzie with "Hugh Wynne — Free Quaker" and Walter D. Edmonds with "Drums Along the Mohawk." McKenzie was a man of rich and varied talent, doctor-artist-historian-novelist; Edmonds knew the history of the Mohawk better than did most historians. His was a clear and compelling story of the agony of the Revolution in that explosive mixture of Loyalist and Patriot that spelled death for the Iroquois confederacy.

While it lasted, the stream of historical romances flowed fast and furiously and then it ceased with startling abruptness. Later on William Lyon Phelps, known to all loyal Yale men as "Billy" Phelps, told a group in the New York Yale Club that the novel that checked the golden flow was one called "The Helmet of Navarre." It was the work of an unskilled young woman and had all the earmarks of the standard model, distressed damsel, clashing swords, high flown terms, but put together clumsily and without charm. Mr. Phelps may well have been right.

A writer of that period who was in no need of constructing an imaginary kingdom for his romancing was Robert W. Chambers. Trained as an artist in a Paris atelier he, too, was drawn to the Mohawk country and turned novelist instead of artist. His characters were found among the retainers, white and Indian, of Sir William Johnson, commissioner of Indian affairs of the British government. Sir William was anxious to hold his Mohawks loyal to the crown, but he dreaded the thought of loosing the tomahawk and scalping knife among the peaceful settlers, a fear which his son John and Walter Butler with the cold pale face did not share. Chambers' books sold well from the start. He began to look away from Indians and settlers, and his success grew. In course of time one of his stories was serialized in a popular magazine. The central figure was a beautiful girl suddenly left alone and penniless who becomes a model for a personable young artist, discovering too late that her duty includes posing in the nude. Of course all ended happily to the music of Lohengrin.

While the serial was running, a young commercial artist was engaged in doing a series of posters for a sporting goods manufacturer in a small town in Connecticut and as a convenience rented a small house in the town. To his surprise he began to receive calls from young ladies of the neighborhood asking if he needed a model. To each caller the artist explained politely that he had no need of female models as his concern was with guns, fishing tackle, canoes, packs and the like, all articles of interest to men only. The calls continued and presently a friend enlightened the puzzled painter: the unwanted models were readers of the Chambers serial. This was something that could never have happened in a world dominated by the great Brahmins.

Around that time, the newspapers of Chicago were a fertile

field for young writers. Such papers as the *Journal*, the *Record*, the *Times'* and the *News*, gave free rein to Eugene Field, Peter Dunne, George Ade, and others. Field died young, only forty-five, but his column "Sharps and Flats" in the *News* had shown the way to other able and resourceful young writers, and there were many to follow the trail he had blazed. His poems of childhood still have much popularity with their sure handling of delicate sentiment and pathos. A surprsing number of these newcomers hailed from Indiana, the special bailiwick of James Whitcomb Riley, the Hoosier poet laureate. It could be said of Riley that he endured his fame, but he did not always enjoy it. A gushing admirer once said to him at a ladies club reception: "Oh, Mr. Riley, is it true that you get a dollar a line for your verse?" Riley replied drily: "Yes, madam, and there are days when I can't think of a damned line."

George Ade, a graduate of Purdue University, wrote his "Fables in Slang" for the old Chicago *Record* and went on to become a playwright with such successful comedies as "The County Chairman," "Just Out of College," and "The College Widow." Ade was the master of a dry wit that never failed him. When he retired to his Indiana farm, a friend asked him what he found to do on a farm after his crowded life in newspaper offices and the theater. His answer was characteristic: "Most of the time I sit on the porch and listen to the hardening of my arteries."

With the multiplication of magazines the market for short stories widened and deepened. The writing of short stories is a special art, a fifty yard dash compared with the leisurely pace of a novel where there is time to shift situations and characters and develop details. Not all writers, even some of the good ones, could qualify, but of those who really made the grade one of the best was William Sidney Porter, pen name "O. Henry." A scornful lady from Boston with a Longfellow somewhere in her family tree dismissed him from notice as "That terrible O. Henry!" If light is needed on that verdict read a chapter from "Cabbages and Kings" and try to imagine a Lowell or a Longfellow lost among the "refugees and consuls" of a mythical Latin American republic where O. Henry was easily at home with supreme disregard for the rules of syntax and structure. The time allotted him was short, but he made good use of it with more than six hundred stories published.

His interest in Latin American themes was of short duration and it was New York that held him in thrall to the end of his life, especially the region around Madison Square and Gramercy Park. In Texas, he had run foul of the law and took a short vacation in federal prison on a charge of embezzlement of postal funds. The memory of this he never lost. In restaurants he sought a table in the most remote corner with his back to the wall. Pan handlers found him an easy touch always good for a dollar or more. To the remonstrance that these were nothing but lazy bums he might reply: "Have you ever been broke and alone? I have."

There was discussion of the identity of his discoverer with honors about even between Bob Davis and Richard Duffy. People like O. Henry are never really discovered; they reveal themselves. He had special tricks which set his stories apart from the run of the mine writer. One of these was reserving the solution for a surprise ending in the last paragraph to the despair of the make-up editor looking for a good place to cut a paragraph or two to fit the space. He found ideas for stories in strange places: a bum sleeping on a park bench might set him off. Once a shop girl in a big department store, underpaid and overworked, gave him the lead for "Piggy." Piggy was a loathsome character whose specialty was preying on shop girls longing for a good dinner and an evening of lights and laughter. O. Henry's shop girl is tempted and about to fall as the action of the piece takes place in her dingy hall bedroom. She has decided to pay the price of her brief moment of pleasure. Pinned to the wall is a newspaper portrait of Kitchener of Khartoum whose grim eyes follow her as she makes her pitiful toilet for sacrifice. "You needn't look at me like that," she says to the portrait. "I'll bet you've never been young and lonely." She turned the print to the wall, but it was no use. She still feels those eyes reproaching her, and in the end it is Kitchener who wins. Such a tale might easily have been mawkish and overwritten, but in O. Henry's sure hands it becomes a jewel.

He was only forty-eight when he died and the manner of his going was in character. As he lay dying in the hospital he gestured feebly to the nurse to raise the window shade and whispered with a hint of a smile a line from a popular song of the day, "I'm afraid to go home in the dark."

Not all the writers of that kaleidoscopic era were writers of fiction. An example was Josiah Flynt, full name Josiah Frank Willard, nephew of the famous temperance advocate Frances E. Willard. Flynt was a man of two sides. He might have been called another Dr. Jekyll and Mr. Hyde if it had been possible to decide which side was Jekyll and which Hyde. In one of his characters he was a member of a highly respectable family, friends of Andrew D. White, sometime president of Cornell University and Ambassador to Russia. In his other role he was a tramp known to his friends of the road as "Cig." His book "Tramping with Tramps" is a classic of sorts. Even in Russia, where he had the entree to the American embassy, he was able to turn tramp for the pleasure of the road.

The final passing of this strange figure was as characteristic as was that of O. Henry. He died alone and unknown in a shabby lodging house in Chicago. There is good reason to conclude that Flynt's favorite role was that of tramp. His clothes were generally old and unpressed and he instinctively shunned bright lights and luxurious surroundings. His favorite hotel in New York was a dingy place somewhere in the neighborhood of West Twelfth Street much frequented by Latin Americans plotting to overthrow the existing regime somewhere south of the border. His choice of a shabby lodging house in Chicago for a hiding place at the end was in character.

A book which provoked much criticism was Edgar Lee Master's "Spoon River Anthology." Was it "creative literature", whatever that means? Was it the paying of an old grudge? Was it the laying of old ghosts? I knew Masters much later in New

York and talked with him often. My conclusion was that it was none of these, or perhaps something of each and something more. Masters had been a student at Knox, but before my time. His home town was Lewistown, Ill., on the Spoon River not far from the Illinois. Lewistown we knew as an old town with old houses and old memories, and something in the place and its past tugged at his coatsleeves and urged him to speak for that past. His speaking was in the name of oldtimers long since dead. It was long since Masters had known the town and he wrote in the interludes of a law practice in Chicago. His Anthology brings to light the hopes, frustrations, dreams, sins of the earlier time.

Naturally Lewistown was displeased and said so. The inscription on the great boulder that marks the grave of Anne Rutledge is taken from the Anthology, but *without credit.* Was Masters paying a grudge or a debt? Perhaps only a writer drawing on his own memories.

An exciting and sometimes controversial figure among the writers of that time was Rudyard Kipling. He was born in India of English parents. His father, John Lockwood Kipling, was an artist and member of the staff of the Mayo School of Industrial Art in Bombay and also of the government museum in that city. Rudyard began writing very young; he was only fifteen when his first sketches appeared in the Lahore *Civil and Military Gazette* and from that time on the tide ran fast, short stories, verses, novels. His fertility was amazing, his success immediate, especially after he settled in England where he fell into the capable hands of a young American, Wolcott Balestier, wise in the ways of London editors and literary agents. Later Kipling married Balestier's sister, but he was never sure that he understood Americans or liked them. He had made that trip to England by way of the Pacific and so across the continent, and had his first look at the United States. In "From Sea to Sea" he records some of his American impressions which were a decidedly mixed lot. In San Francisco, he saw a prostitute with the face of one of Botticelli's angels and suffered long after-dinner ora-

tory in honor of a young naval lieutenant who had been deco-
rated for conspicuous gallantry in a hurricane at Samoa. The
young lieutenant delivered him from his weariness by stam-
mering through a few disjointed sentences, concluding with
"What I say is give us more ships!" "He was a man," said Kipling. He saw the wonders of Yellowstone and talked with one
of the cavalrymen then acting as park guards. The small horses
puzzled him and he asked the trooper if he thought American
cavalry could stand up to heavy European dragoons. The soldier's answer gave him to think. "We wouldn't try," said the
young man. "We'd just lay behind rocks and trees and shoot
'em out of their saddles." Kipling remembered this when he
saw Canadian and Australian mounted riflemen in South Africa
during the Boer War.

Somewhere, in Omaha perhaps, he talked with a maker of
caskets and burial clothes for the late lamented. He learned
that standard American practice permitted the providing of back-
less gowns and coats and made rueful comment on the plight of
the unhappy spirits walking backward around heaven through
all eternity. The Chicago stockyards drew him as they did other
visitors, particularly Europeans, and he found there just what
might be expected in a slaughter house, blood, evil smells, and
the clanking of the engines of death.

He reports with the air of a worshiper sitting at the feet
of Mark Twain in the Elmira home where he found him. There's
something wrong here. Albert Bigelow Paine in his life of Clemens writes that the Clemens family had no recollection of such
a call until a young daughter of the house produced a card that
had been left on a hall table and that she had saved because of
the strangeness of the inscription: Rudyard Kipling, Alahabad
Pioneer. Ah well! Even Homer limped.

Kipling brought with him to the Western world a treasure
of the East greater than any that Clive or Warren Hastings knew,
"Soldiers Three," "Plain Tales from the Hills," "Stories of Mine
Own People." As Mark Twain had revealed to us the romance
and adventure of our own West, this newcomer made known to

us facets of the Anglo-Indian life as has not been done before or since. Not all of our editors responded to this opportunity, but McClure and his kind understood and reaped a harvest.

Kipling's field in prose was the short story. His experiments with novels were not happy, although "Kim" should be named as an exception. In this book a half caste boy wise with the wisdom of the streets and the native quarters, speaking native dialects, and knowing all the superstitions and taboos, wove a magic tapestry of which he was a part. Another milieu in which Kipling was not fortunate was in the portrayal of women. His women were too often hard-eyed dabblers in adultery or shallow simpering dispensers of baby talk. Kipling's world was the world of men in which he moved with assurance. He had a mastery of the patois of crafts and trades and he made few slips. His study and presentation of incidental details was thorough as can be seen in his long poems, "McAndrew's Hymn" and the "Mary Gloster," and to a less extent in "Captains Courageous." A wandering young American who was a worshipper at the Kipling Shrine told the poet once of a cruise from Ceylon to Australia in a tramp steamer whose captain was also a Kipling fan. One day the skipper told the American that they were passing near a spot in the Indian Ocean named by the poet in "Mary Gloster" with latitude, longitude, and depth and set his course to come to the same position; "118 East and South just 3." A sounding confirmed the Kipling line. Kipling made sarcastic comment: "So you thought a blue nosed Yankee and a tramp skipper could trap me when I have a set of deep sea charts at hand!"

In both prose and verse Kipling's was the voice of British imperialism calling particular attention to the part played by the common soldier. Any of the stories in "Soldiers Three" will illustrate this as will many verses:

> Then it's Tommy this an' Tommy that an' Tommy
>   'ow's yer soul,
> But it's thin red line of 'eroes w'en the drums begin
>   to roll.

Any writer who turns out as many pages of print as did
this man is bound to do some things that are below average.
There was "If" for example. To this amateur critic there was a
flavor of Tin Pan Alley about it, a kind of jingling pomposity:

> If you can keep your head when all about you
> Men are losing theirs and blaming it on you;
> If you can trust yourself when all men doubt you,
> And make allowance for the doubting too,
> If you can fill each unforgiving minute
> With sixty seconds worth of distance run,
> Yours is the earth and everything that's in it
> And which is more you'll be a man, my son.

Tin Pan Alley or not, "If" was voted the favorite poem with
many graduating classes in American colleges.

Along with his praise of the England he saw from overseas — "little they know of England who only England know" —
and his drum beat of empire around the world, there were signs
that even the stately ceremonial of the Jubilee roused in him an
uneasiness of mind and a hint of doom. Read his famous "Reces-
sional" that found its way into patriotic hymnals:

> Far called our navies melt away,
> On dune and headland sink the fires,
> Lo, all our pomp of yesterday
> Is one with Nineveh and Tyre's.

It was his good fortune to die before the liquidation of the empire
that he had praised so lustily, but it is not impossible that he felt
the stirring of a doubt deep in him.

Perhaps Kipling was the last of the famous English writers
to exhibit familiarity with the Bible, sometimes by the turn of a
phrase, sometimes by direct allusion. A case in point is this line
from "Gentlemen Rankers," "For the curse of Reuben holds us
till an alien turf enfolds us . . . " Who was Reuben and what
was his curse? The answer will be found in the book of Genesis,
Chapter 49. Reuben was the first born son of Jacob and a great
disappointment to his father and this was his curse, "Unstable
as water thou shalt not excel."

Kipling found our country large and shambling, not at all like England. We were too much given to loud boasting and squabbling in the marketplace, but we had some of the makings and something might be done for us yet. The American Spirit speaks:

> Enslaved, illogical, elate,
> He greets the embarrassed gods, nor fears
> To shake the iron hand of Fate
> Or match with Destiny for beers.
> Lo; Imperturbable he rules,
> Unkempt, disreputable, vast —
> And in the teeth of all the schools
> I — I shall save him at the last.

Lecture bureaus and agents cast wistfully hopeful glances at Kipling and sought to tempt him to try the golden path of an American tour. It was a waste of time. He was committed to the craft of the writer and had no appetite for the rigors of the road. There is recollection of only two Kipling speeches, one on his induction as chancellor of the University of Aberdeen which was a frank admonition to his young hearers to drink only in moderation and gamble only for such sums as the players could afford to lose.

The other speech was delivered at a Royal Academy dinner. This was pure Kiplingese. The scene is in a prehistoric cave. The men of the tribe have returned from the hunt and essay in grunts and gurgles to tell of the killing of the mighty sabre-toothed tiger. Then appears one who has the gift of words. He tells of the adventure as he saw it unfold and the listeners thrill to the drama, their blood runs cold to the danger and they exult over the triumph. But some of the wiser men are disturbed by the spectacle. This man has magic, they declare. He is dangerous; and they fall upon him with clubs and stones and kill him. "And that," Kipling concluded, "was the first authentic example of constructive criticism."

An incidental note of the rising chorus of literary expression of that time was struck by a curious medley of hope, aspiration, and here and there of shrewd publicity. Perhaps a time of rapid change produces its own lunatic fringe of expression. Emerson had noted such a ferment in his time. Of the Charndon Street Convention called by the Friends of Universal Reform he wrote: "If the assembly was disorderly it was picturesque. Mad men, mad women, men with beards, Dunkers, Muggletonians, Come Outers, Groaners, Agrarians, Seventh Day Baptists, Quakers, Abolitionists, Calvinists, Unitarians, and Philosophers, — all came successively to the top and seized their day, if not their hour, in which to chide, or pray, or protest."

Emerson was amused also by the tendency to seek some magic phrase or technique by which mankind might lift itself by its bootstraps. Our time had examples of such magic makers. One was Emil Coue who came out with his proposal of a species of autohypnotism by repeated assertion of the phrase "Every day in every way I am getting better and better." Pastor Wagner wrote a little book in praise of the Simple Life; of this it might be said that it was a good trick if you could do it. Another genius much later reaped a considerable harvest with his program. "How to Make Friends and Influence People." Still later a clergyman on Fifth Avenue packed the house with his sermons on the "Power of Right Thinking." Of this a light-minded critic suggested a couple of logical variants, the "Power of Wrong Thinking" and the "Power of Not Thinking at All."

The man who dominated this tumultuous scene was Elbert Hubbard, the "Sage of East Aurora," in his way a genius. He had a printing plant which he called the Roycrofters and he founded a magazine the *Philistine* and he really cut something of a swath. He was a shrewd judge of publicity values and he made his books printed on deckle-edged paper and bound in limp leather, a badge of culture. All a young man in a small apartment needed to prove himself a man of culture, was a Morris chair and a small shelf of Roycroft books, most of which Hubbard wrote himself. His chef d'oeuvre was a Message to Garcia. This was a highly inspirational number. A major — name forgotten — is sent with a message to Garcia who is heading an insurrection somewhere in the middle of Cuba. It was a routine assignment involving little effort but a slight element of danger, the sort of thing that army men are familiar with — or should be. The message was duly delivered but the incident set the Sage to thinking and he turned out a screed consisting mostly of the things that might have happened but didn't. This caught the eye of "Uncle" George H. Daniels, general passenger agent of the New York Central lines, and he made a brochure of it and mailed it out to all his agents for their edification and encouragement, and there was another feather in the cap of the Sage. Hubbard's career ended tragically when he and his wife went down with the *Lusitania*.

CHAPTER XIII

THE GATHERING CLOUDS

AS THE world moved on into the new century signs and portents multiplied. The British Empire was old and experienced, set in its ways. The East India Company had been founded a few years before the colony of Virginia and before the middle of the eighteenth century large fortunes were being made in the trade with India. The British ruled the waves — all the waves there were. They had the ships and the treaty ports and were superb traders.

In general the Pax Brittanica was a peace of order and of law. By the turn of the century the British were apparently firmly established on the China Coast, in India and Malaya; Singapore was the Gibraltar of the East, invulnerable against attack on all sides — except the side from which the attack would ultimately come; South Africa was a British bonanza, diamonds, gold, copper, land. East Africa was also British with farmers rivaling big game hunters.

After the Franco - Prussian war, France had turned to her colonies in Algiers for solace for her lost colonies of Alsace and Lorraine. Bismarck had exacted an indemnity from France that he thought would "bleed her white for a generation." The French paid it almost over night. In the new German Empire the restless young Kaiser had dropped the old chancellor over the side — Sir John Tenniel's cartoon in *Punch* "Dropping the Pilot" is a historic document — and set about overtaking Britain. Britain had dominated the world with her navy, her merchant marine, and her colonies. Very well, he would follow her example, but where? He found a naval base in China, but it was in a weak spot and could never be the germ of a colony. He picked up a few unconsidered islands in the Pacific and matched Britain in East Africa with a German East Africa, mostly primitive jungle, no gold or diamonds. Clearly Germany was overlooking something. All the German colonists found was wars with naked savages such as the Hereroes while the British found peace and profit.

Bismarck held stubbornly to his belief that the future of Germany lay in the east and southeast — *drang nach osten* — with a railroad from Berlin to Bagdad. There was trade enough to be found there and there was no reason for matching ships and colonies with the British. But the old pilot had been dropped, a young Kaiser was at the helm and Germany was putting out to sea with dreadnaughts and merchant ships with luxury liners to boot.

An American in London in 1912 was troubled when he heard English friends say, "*When* we fight Germany." "Is it as bad as that?" he asked. The answers varied little. Germany was trying to match the British in naval power and must be taught a lesson. Of course it would be a short war, a naval battle or two, no British troops on the Continent and Germany would surrender. The war came but it was not a short war nor was it limited to the sea. Before it ended Englishmen, Americans, Canadians, Australians, Italians, Gurkhas from remote India, South Africans, the races of the world fought alongside the French and the Belgians. The total casualties of all the belligerent powers in this "short war" were in excess of thirty-seven and a half million, the greatest blood bath the world had yet known.

Of course none of this was evident in the early years of the new century. We had had the brief flurry of our war with Spain, but in general we took peace for granted. Our biggest war had been in our own back yard and Europe since 1815 had fought only limited liability wars, short and simple, Franco-Prussian, the two-week war between Prussia and Austria, the short scuffle by which Prussia and Austria had taken the Schleswig-Holstein area from Denmark. To be sure there was a long bushwhacking dispute with unhappy natives in the Dutch East Indies, occasional affairs along the Afghan border involving a regiment or two to root out snipers in the hills, skirmishes with head-hunters in Borneo, but these were only the inevitable incidents that colonial empires such as Britain and Holland must expect, part of the white man's burden.

In the United States many people were unhappy over our position in the Philippines. Emilio Aguinaldo had declared a Philippine Republic and to some the reasonable step after beating Spain was recognition of this regime as the legitimate government and the withdrawal of our troops as speedily as possible. That was considered and our first relations with Aguinaldo were friendly enough, but Admiral Dewey advised against such action on the ground that Aguinaldo's support was factional and unreliable. Another possibility was to hold the island of Luzon which contained Manila and turn the rest of the archipelago over to the rebels. There was a vague but highly emotional objection to "hauling down the flag" and a strong but mostly unspoken argument on the ground of the rich profit in trade with the Filipinos. In the end the president decided that there "was nothing left for us to do but to take them all, and to educate the Filipinos and uplift and Christianize them."

After our victory over Spain and our uneasy acquisition of the Philippines we were not long in learning that our new position on the borders of the China Sea was not all beer and skittles. We had paid Spain $20,000,000 for her interest in the archipelago and a dubious interest in a flourishing rebellion. Spain had been easy meat but Aguinaldo kept us busy for four years. If this was part of the white man's burden an increasing number of us wanted no part of it, but we were in the islands and we didn't know how to get out. The Imperialists were sounding the tocsin of empire and American business was still dreaming of fat profits in trade with the little brown brother who was behaving in a most unbrotherly manner.

And that wasn't all of our worries in the Far East. Li Hung

Chang had set out to create a modern Chinese navy that had clashed with the Japanese in a brief naval war in 1894-5 and at the end of it there was no Chinese navy, but there was a growing anti-foreign movement in China. Germany was hungry for trade and territory on the China coast that might match the British grip on Hong Kong. To the north the Russians pushed farther into Manchuria with the extending of the TransSiberian railway.

Into this delicate situation the Chinese launched an anti-foreign movement, known to us as the Boxer Rebellion, in China "The Order of Literary Patriotic Harmonious Fists." Dislike of the foreign devils had been endemic in China for generations. In many minds there was a cynical sequence that ran thus: First the missionary with his Bible; then the trader with his bales of goods; finally the gunboat with the flag. Now with Germany crowding in to rival the British and the Japanese looking with hungry eyes at the Russians in Manchuria trouble began to boil up. Americans might be friendly for the time being but how long would it be before they too grew greedy for trade and bases? Chinese undercover leaders began to mutter about China for the Chinese. And why not? Chinese civilization was old, the oldest in the world, and what need had they for something called the true religion? Christianity seemed a discordant medley, Protestant, Catholic, Methodist, Presbyterian, Baptist, Seventh Day Adventist, competing with each other, quarreling among themselves. Was that Christianity? Chinese religions were old, Confucian, Buddhist, Shintoist, but they lived at peace with each other which was more than these Christians seemed willing to do. The crafty "Old Empress" was ostensibly friendly to foreigners but watchfully waiting on events.

The Boxers struck first in outlying points, isolated mission posts, burning, killing. Elsewhere cautious teachers and preachers yearned increasingly for the comfort and security of the homeland as the sense of dedication to a cause grew dim. The streets and compounds ceased to beckon to foreign tourists and seekers after native curios and artifacts.

The movement came to a head when armed mobs attacked

the sacred embassy buildings and embassy staffs readied themselves to withstand a siege. This was something more than a local ferment and the European powers called for joint action, this time enlisting American help, ultimately five thousand men, mostly marines. The Kaiser strutted into the glare of the spotlight, adjuring his troops to so bear themselves that for a thousand years Chinese mothers would quiet their fretful children with tales of the terrible Huns. Here was a forecast of things to come if the rest of the world had had the wit to understand.

The troops landed at Tientsin, the port of Peking, and started the march to the imperial city. It was a tough eighty miles with sporadic fighting all the way, but the besieged legations were relieved and an uneasy peace settled down. There was a disgraceful aftermath with alleged Christians looting the imperial palace and coming away loaded with priceless articles, tapestry, furs, coats covered with gold and silver brocade. Bad as this was it was small compared with the official indemnity of $330,000,000 demanded for the injured feelings of the civilized powers. The share allotted to the Americans was $24,000,000, but we had the grace to take only the amount necessary to cover actual damage to legation property, turning the balance back to the Chinese to help defray the expenses of Chinese students in the United States.

John Hay, our wise Secretary of State, seized the opportunity to approach the European powers with his proposal for an Open Door to China:

> The policy of the government of the United States is to seek a solution which may bring about permanent peace and safety to China, preserve Chinese territorial and administrative entity, protect all rights guaranteed to friendly powers by treaty and international law and safeguard for the world the principle of equal and impartial trade with all parts of the Chinese Empire.

Only the British showed genuine interest expressing their willingness to go along if the others would agree. Germans, Russians, and Japanese did little more than acknowledge the receipt of the communication.

In the closing years of the eighteenth century an English clergyman Thomas R. Malthus had come out with a book that carried a solemn warning. Malthus had been studying the relation of population to food supply and had reached the conclusion that population tended to increase in geometrical ratio while the supply of food grew only arithmetically. As a result mankind was heading inevitably toward starvation. This Malthusian doctrine might well have given Thomas Carlyle reason for the term "gloomy science" that he hung on the study of economics. Very little attention was paid to the theorizing of the Rev. Mr. Malthus. The world had known famine as well as war and pestilence and still the number of people in the world grew greater.

In reality Malthus's warning was only premature. At the time when he was writing the world was on the threshold of a period of tremendous increase of the area available for the production of food. The young United States was beginning to move away from the Atlantic seaboard to find new land in the wilderness of Ohio, but our western boundary was still the Mississippi River. Thomas Jefferson was the only statesman who dared dream of a farther west, perhaps even to the "Western Ocean." For most Americans the lands beyond the great Mississippi were fit only for wild beasts and wilder men, both red and white. Spain — or was it France? — seated at the mouth of the river claimed the sovereignty of a vague empire called the Louisiana Territory. Soon Jefferson was to make his crazy purchase of an empire from France and send Merriwether Lewis and William Clark to have a look at the new acquisition but it would be a long time before Daniel Webster would be convinced that wheels would ever roll across the Rockies. In spite of Mr. Webster the new nation was beginning to grow and would soon stretch from sea to sea, more than twice as large an area under one government as men had thought possible when the Founding Fathers argued through the hot summer in Philadelphia.

There is a historical footnote here that is not without interest. Alexander Hamilton had little hope for the new government. After the Constitution had been ratified he spoke of it as a frail reed that could hardly outlast the time of men then living. In 1831 John Quincy Adams recorded in his diary his belief that the only hope for survival was to divide the continental expanse into at least three governments; otherwise he gave the United States not more than ten years, perhaps only five.

Africa had been a land of mystery and danger through much of recorded history. Egypt and Carthage were old when Rome was young, but the rest of the continent was a blank in most of the school geographies until late in the nineteenth century. Bennett, the owner of the New York *Herald*, sent Henry M. Stanley to find David Livingston, missionary, explorer, adventurer, supposed to be lost somewhere in the jungles of the Dark Continent. Livingston didn't know he was lost and the manner of his finding got into Stanley's autobiography. The correspondent gave formal greeting: "Dr. Livingston, I presume. My name is Stanley." Africa was in the blood of both men and Stanley after reporting his success returned to find the way across to the west coast. Then in 1877 he came down the Congo to salt water and Africa had been opened.

Malthus died in 1834 still believing in the accuracy of his calculation of the gloomy ratio of population to food supply. For most of us the more our population grew the better we liked it. Our cities counted heads and we boasted smugly of our superiority over our rivals. Our municipal governments were inept and often corrupt but growth in our numbers was the all important fact. We were proud of the story told by our decennial census reports — 1800, 5,308,483; a hundred and fifty years later, 150,-697,161.

For years, centuries even, men had been pushing and probing their way into the savage corners of the world and especially the polar regions, Arctic and Antarctic. As that first decade of the new century wore away there seemed a greater urgency in the search for Latitude 90 as though to clear the way for impending events, and in 1909 Robert Peary crowned the effort of a lifetime by reaching the North Pole. Close on the word of his success came a rival claimant, a Dr. Frederick Cook, and what should have been an occasion for rejoicing turned into a disgraceful hassle. I talked with both men and retain a clear impression of their personalities. Peary, the dedicated professional, was tense as a coiled spring, bitterly resentful that an unknown interloper should dare to claim the prize for which he, Peary, had worked and studied and trained. Cook, by contrast, was relaxed, almost casual. He had little to say of equipment or method, only that he had found the weather mild and with a stray Eskimo had strolled to the Pole. How had he determined his position? There too he was vague and one cynical commentator remarked that he had carried an Ingersoll watch for the purpose and that his food supply seemed to consist of mostly of a bag of gumdrops.

To the hardheaded realists the odds were all on Peary but Cook had many friends and Peary many enemies. It should be said that Cook was a good companion in camp and on the trail carrying more than his share of the load and always cheerful and communicative. Peary, on the other hand, made few friends and said as little as possible. On his way back to Newfoundland after his trip to the Pole he told no one of the outcome of his effort; even Macmillan his long time associate was left to guess. Another point against Peary was that his only companion on the final march was his Negro valet.

Apparently the air of individualistic America is favorable to something that might be called the amateur spirit, the quality that has enabled us to conquer the continent from sea to sea and bind it with railroads. We wanted to believe that it was easy to reach the Pole if one gave his mind to it so there were loud cheers for Cook, the amateur.

Cook's case was too thin to withstand the challenge of skilled investigators and he dropped from sight to reappear briefly as the promoter of a shady scheme for bringing together a number of dry wells in a Texas oil field, on the theory apparently that nothing added to nothing equals something. The court disagreed with his arithmetic and Cook went to Leavenworth prison.

How does one explain such a man as Cook? Why did he make such a claim without at least some evidence beyond a feeble statement? A man who had camped with him and climbed with him in a try at the summit of Mt. McKinley said of him that he was a high financier among explorers. Perhaps that says it.

Three years later the South Pole was reached by Capt. Robert Scott an Englishman and the manner of it was pure tragedy. Scott brought a number of hardy Siberian ponies and three or four motor sledges for transport over the high plateau that guards the Pole. As the polar party of five approached their goal they found disturbing signs, ski and sledge tracks and footprints of dogs, sure proof that Scott and his men were late. They reached the Pole to find a Norwegian flag flying that had been hoisted only a month before by Roald Amundsen. It was the return march that was to prove deadly for the Englishmen, a total of more than eight hundred and fifty miles under man power only, no more motor sledges, ponies or dogs. Now the weather turned foul and where a month earlier the Norwegians had traveled fast on skis, Scott and his men faced punishing gales and low temperatures so that many days were lost and progress was painfully slow.

The tragic story was told in Scott's journal which was found lying on his body when the relief party under Dr. Atkinson came up nearly eight months later. His Message to the Public gave eloquent testimony to their struggle. "We are weak, writing is difficult, but for my own sake I do not regret this journey, which has shown that Englishmen can endure hardships, help one another, and meet death with as great a fortitude as ever in the past. Had we lived I should have had a tale to tell of the hardihood, courage and endurance of my companions which would have stirred the heart of every Englishman." The bodies were buried under a cairn of snow and ice and two skis lashed in the form of of a cross held this inscription: "To seek, to strive, to find, and not to yield."

There was another act of heroism in the record. Captain Oates' feet were so badly frozen that he could barely hobble. He

had urged his comrades to leave him as a worthless helpless in-
cumbrance. Finally in this camp of death he had struggled to his
feet with the remark: "I am going outside. I may be gone sometime." Then he had shuffled out into the raging blizzard. For
him there was another inscription: "Hereabouts died a very gal-
lant gentleman."

Another tragedy of that fateful year was the sinking of the
White Star liner *Titanic* on her maiden voyage. The *Titanic* had
been loudly heralded as the largest — 882½ feet long — unsink-
able, the queen of the seas bound to make a new record in westward crossing. There had been warning of icebergs ahead but
she slammed into the flank of a large berg at full speed and went
down carrying more than fifteen hundred people with her.

Then on June 28, 1914, in Bosnia, a province of Serbia, an
obscure student, one Gravillo Prinzip, killed the Archduke Francis Ferdinand, heir to the Austrian throne, and his wife. Austria
attacked Serbia, Germany came to the aid of Austria, Russia mo-
bilized her army to support the Serbs, Germany declared that
the joint treaty guaranteeing the neutrality of Belgium was after
all only a "scrap of paper" as she sent her armies through Belgium to strike at France and Britain sprang to the side of France,
her traditional enemy. Our peaceful world became a battlefield
in the space of a fortnight. Three years later America came in.
Fifty years later we are still reaping the bitter harvest of war.